Cherished

Devotions of Love and Hope

Teresa Ann Winton

Cherished: Devotions of Love and Hope
Copyright © 2023 Teresa Ann Winton. All rights reserved.

No part of this book may be reproduced in any form or by any electronic or mechanical means, including information storage and retrieval systems, without permission in writing from the author, except by reviewers, who may quote brief passages in a review.

Scripture taken from:
NEW AMERICAN STANDARD BIBLE®,
Copyright © 1960,1962,1963,1968,1971,1972,1973,1975,1977,1995
by The Lockman Foundation. Used by permission.
ESV® Bible (The Holy Bible, English Standard Version®), copyright © 2001 by Crossway, a publishing ministry of Good News Publishers. Used by permission. All rights reserved.
Holy Bible, King James Version, Cambridge 1769. Public domain.

ISBN: 978-1-7344627-3-9

Cover design by Ian Winton and Angie Alaya
Interior design and layout by Ian Winton
Editing by Ian Winton

Dedication

To you, Ian, my dearly loved son.
And to Ricky, Rachael, Charlotte, Freddie,
and the memory of Tracy and Tim.

Acknowledgments

I'd like to thank God—my eternal Father—Whose grace and love have saved me and given me a home in His ever-abiding heart. All praise goes to Him for helping me to find beauty from the ashes and wisdom in writing these devotions.

Ian, you are a profound blessing and have been essential in putting this book together. Thank you for your design contribution and insight on the cover, and the beautiful work you've done in formatting and designing the interior. I could not have done this without your exquisite talent! Your opulent eye for detail is a gift God has given. I pray the wisdom contained in this book will strengthen, encourage, and comfort you. The memories we've shared in designing my books are a treasure dear to my heart. You are the best part of my life; forever loved and cherished!

My sincerest regards to my devoted friends—you have been my family and have remained supportive, kind, and true. Some of you have remained dear friends as far back as my days in foster care. You were family back then and you are today!

Angie, thank you for helping to bring to life our design concept for the cover. We could not have done this without your expertise and skill.

I wish to also thank my Facebook followers, friends, and fans for buying my books and remaining loyal readers throughout my writing career.

I am forever grateful to those who have mentored and inspired me to find pearls of wisdom in God's Word, and grace in the cross of our LORD Jesus Christ.

Table of Contents

Our Home..1
There is a Place of Quiet Rest....................................7
God's Understanding is Infinite.................................8
When Tears Fail..12
Abide With Me..18
I'll Carry You...19
God Will Take Care of You.......................................23
Crushed and Broken...24
Whispering Hope..44
Beautiful Evergreen..45
Wings...49
Dimly Burning..52
Words and Thoughts..55
Scared of the Spider...58
Our Safe House...62
Tender Regard..68
Solace in Sorrow...73
Sweet By and By...78
Tears Took Your Soul...81
Angelic Comfort...82
Seal Upon His Heart..88
Tender Mercies..92
The Sands of Time are Sinking..............................100
Face of Light...101
Holy, Holy, Holy!..105

Contrite Heart	106
Whisper of God	108
Can We Start Over?	112
Letters Before God	116
Beautiful World	120
This Is My Father's World	125
Gift of Dawn and Twilight	126
We Will Meet Again	129
Wistful Portraits	132
Fountain of Youth	134
Providential Gifts	137
Eternal Friendship	140
Empathy	145
To Belong	149
Cherished and Chosen	153
Permanent	157
Loyal Love	162
Psalm 103	167
No Night There	168
Coming Home	169

Our Home

And He walks with me, and He talks with me,
And He tells me I am His own.
—C. Austin Miles

He who dwells in the shelter of the Most High
will abide in the shadow of the Almighty.
I will say to the LORD, 'My refuge and my fortress,
my God, in whom I trust.'
—Psalm 91:1-2

We will encounter seasons of personal discouragement and feelings of hopelessness. Tragic events, personal failures, and losses can leave us feeling bewildered and powerless, yearning for an escape. Where can we go and what can we do when the walls of our world begin to fall and there doesn't seem to be an end in sight, or a respite of comfort?

I recently found myself needing a serene place to refresh my spirit. God was my sheltering place—hearth and home—where I could leave my sorrows behind and step into serenity with Him. My son and I designed a special garden where we could have family and devotional gatherings to inspire our hearts; the fluttering butterflies and birds singing lullabies soothed our souls in the wafting floral breezes.

God is our Father of Lights; the source and the everlasting Fountain of all light. He has adorned our world with radiance in the sky—the sun, the moon, and the stars. His light is exquisite, an all-encompassing Light of our earthly world, as well as the heavenly celestial Light Who longs to take us into His bosom. Our Creator is the emblem of Holiness and perfection, lacking nothing.

> *Every good thing given and every perfect gift is*
> *from above, coming down from the Father of Lights,*
> *with Whom there is no variation*
> *or shifting shadow.*
> —James 1:17

When our way is unsteady and our minds are ravaged with worry, we can find stability in our Father because He doesn't change. And even though God doesn't need us, He still treats each of us as dear treasure who needs to be guarded and protected. He is our magnificent Home of Light and we are His children with an inheritance.

> *The Spirit Himself testifies with our spirit*
> *that we are children of God, and if children,*
> *heirs also, heirs of God and fellow heirs with Christ,*
> *if indeed we suffer with Him so that we may also be*
> *glorified with Him.*
> —Romans 8:16-17

Psalm 121:4 reads: *Behold, He Who keeps Israel will neither slumber nor sleep.* God is always up and available! Even when we crash and fall, God is there as our Beacon at all times!

> *For a day in Your courtyards*
> *is better than a thousand elsewhere.*
> —Psalm 84:10

David was a man acquainted with royalty and could have whatever he desired, yet in the Scripture above, he expressed his genuine joy, reverence, and preference for the LORD'S house. And just like David, we, too, would find more happiness and true joy in one day spent in the heart of God than a thousand days spent elsewhere.

In God's courts, we meet with God the King, and are assured of comfort, enlightenment, and blessings through Christ, our Mediator. One day we'll all face the last moment of our lives; it will be the sweetest memories and those spent in Holiness and communication with God, our Creator and Father, that will matter the most. As long as there's breath, we can go to the House of God, commune, and worship Him, and then die saved in His arms.

Isaiah 40:28 reads: *Do you not know? Have you not heard? The Everlasting God, the LORD, the Creator of the ends of the earth does not become weary or tired. His understanding is unsearchable.* Since God cannot grow weary or faint, He is our ultimate source for renewing our spirits when we are distraught and depleted.

*When I'm weary, weak, and sad,
His serene wings unfurl and hold me close.*

We are revived when we surrender our baggage at the feet of our LORD. It's not until we let it all go—emptying our soul in the presence of God Almighty—that we find complete rest. Getting quiet with the LORD allows us to be sensitive to the inner working of the Holy Spirit.

Can you think of a time when you were invited to a dear friend's house and they doted on you so much that you were shown all their treasures and trinkets, and then left with an arm load of them to take home? And were you so deeply cherished that you knew there was nothing they wouldn't do for you, or give to you, if it were within their power to do so? God, too, longs to bestow us with His relentless, extravagant love, and timeless treasures through a Holy relationship in Him.

Most of us have framed photos of our dear ones hanging on our walls or sitting on our furniture. These treasured keepsakes help us to feel close to those we love. In a spiritual sense, we can also have mementos of our LORD to treasure. Since we cannot see or touch God, we can envision Him in a framed collage hanging on the wall of our heart. Just as a photo of a family member or friend brings us comfort and cheer, we can also find comfort and inspiration by spending time with God. Each time we discover another lovely attribute of the LORD, we can add it to the lonely and unfulfilled places of our heart—in time, that will fill the rooms of our souls with the timeless beauty of the LORD.

> *Seek the LORD, and His strength;*
> *seek His face evermore.*
> *—Psalm 105:4*

Our God is a harbor, where we step beyond the troubled sea of our souls onto a paradise path. There on the rose marble threshold, He waits to kiss our cheeks, wrap us in His arms, and whisper, 'Welcome Home—in Me—find rest for your souls.'

> *Come to Me, all who are weary and burdened,*
> *and I will give you rest.*
> *—Matthew 11:28*

Within this book are devotions, poems, and hymns meant to inspire, encourage, and comfort as you go through life with its sundry troubles. Run to God and don't try to bear it alone. God will lead you in the path of life as He stills and refreshes your soul with wisdom and solutions for the problems threatening your peace.

> *You make known to me the path of life;*
> *in Your presence there is fullness of joy;*
> *at Your right hand are pleasures forevermore.*
> *—Psalm 16:11*

In His presence you will experience absolute and lasting joy. God longs to bless you with not only pleasure now, but in ways the human mind cannot fathom on this side of Heaven. God does not faint or grow weary, but we do. We must tap into God's Spirit and take on Jesus' rest—His joy, and His everlasting strength—if we are to live balanced and refreshed. God's Word is our escape from this troubled world and all that burdens.

If this world, and its chaos, disappointments, and sorrows have taken a toll on you and you don't know what to do, and finding a solution is taxing your reserves, I invite you to open the pages of this book and find love, hope, comfort, and the timeless wisdom of God. His Heart is our place to find centering for our lives, joy, inspiration, and serenity for our souls.

> *Blessed be the God and Father*
> *of our LORD Jesus Christ,*
> *the Father of mercies and God of all comfort,*
> *Who comforts us in all our affliction*
> *so that we will be able to comfort those*
> *who are in any affliction*
> *with the comfort with which we ourselves*
> *are comforted by God.*
> *—2 Corinthians 1:3-4*

There is a Place of Quiet Rest

There is a place of quiet rest,
Near to the heart of God;
A place where sin cannot molest,
Near to the heart of God.

There is a place of comfort sweet,
Near to the heart of God;
A place where we our Savior meet,
Near to the heart of God.

There is a place of full release,
Near to the heart of God;
A place where all is joy and peace,
Near to the heart of God.

O Jesus, blest Redeemer,
Sent from the heart of God;
Hold us, who wait before Thee,
Near to the heart of God.

—Cleland Boyd McAfee

God's Understanding is Infinite

Having someone to understand us is paramount when we're weary with troubles. Many of us will face burdens greater than a human friend can carry. And it won't be because they don't try to understand, but because they can't. We don't have to despair that there's no one to whom we can turn when our troubles consume us. God makes Himself available unceasingly. His intelligence on any issue or crisis has no bounds. He can do all things and knows all things; who could be a more worthy confidant than God?

His understanding is infinite.
—Psalm 147:5

God's mercy—His steadfast love—is as far reaching as the heavens are above the earth. What I love about this aspect of our Father is that He doesn't have to hear the back story or research potential solutions; He is already there in the complexities of our lives where we are fully known. A more faithful friend does not exist, nor can any grasp the power of God.

> *For Your steadfast love is great to the heavens,*
> *Your faithfulness to the clouds.*
> —Psalm 57:10

At times the answers don't come right away, but we gain comfort and strength from communing with God, and the comfort and strength continues to soothe as we call on the LORD. God's timing is never off, so when we wait patiently in faith, He'll come through in impeccable and supernatural ways; we can count on it.

When we are in distress and darkness, God will send His Light if only we trust and ask Him. God's being is light and He'll lead us to His Holy face where we can worship in spirit and truth, and where we can find tranquility for our mind and cleansing for our heart. His truth will take away confusion, allowing clarity and discernment. We'll then find the courage to take action if it's needed, or to peacefully accept what we cannot change. God keeps His promises and will fulfill every need in His perfect timing.

> *Send out Your light and Your truth,*
> *they shall lead me;*
> *they shall bring me to Your Holy hill*
> *and to Your dwelling places.*
> —Psalm 43:3

The LORD Jesus is the Sun of Righteousness; the promised Messiah, our hope. His ray of light enlightens, inspires, heals, and refines our soul through His grace and spirit. Christ is our Advocate Who radiates blessings from one end of Heaven to the other. Those of us who believe on His name go out with grace; we are full of life, satisfied and joyful, like happy, playful calves just released from their stall.

> *But for you who fear My name,*
> *the Sun of righteousness will rise*
> *with healing in its wings;*
> *and you will go forth and frolic*
> *like calves from the stall.*
> *—Malachi 4:2*

> *The LORD is my rock, and my fortress,*
> *and my deliverer;*
> *my God, my strength, in Whom I will trust;*
> *my buckler, and the horn of my salvation,*
> *and my high tower.*
> *—Psalm 18:2*

King David recognized the LORD as his Rock—his shelter from men and dangerous animals. David found strength and safety in this fortress and escape from whatever troubled him. He was saved from his enemies on many occasions.

We read in 1 Samuel 13:14 that David was a man after *God's own heart*. Obviously David was not infallible, but he deeply adored God and took great comfort knowing God as the Fountain from Whom all his good would come. And an inexhaustible fountain at that! He relied upon God as his shield, his defender, Who kept him safe physically and with spiritual discernment in his heart. God was his high tower Who allowed him to see the country around him before danger could approach.

Our family and friends can become weary, but not God. He is our Rock of protection and our heavenly Counselor. We can find strength through His Fortress because He is our Protector, Helper, Friend, Father, and Savior. And like King David, we can confide in Him and have assurance that He will guard and protect the contents of our hearts.

God is our castle where our enemies can't reach and where we can heal, work through troubles, and find ultimate comfort for our souls. When He designed us, He took into account all hardships and struggles we'd face. He put in each of us the courage, strength, talent, and wisdom to overcome them all and to become all that we were meant to be. No matter what comes our way, we are not alone; God is beside us, holding us up and close to His breast. Like David, we can also grow in the likemindedness of God as we pursue His heart.

Keep pressing forward, holding onto God's wings;
Serenity is on its way, it will soon greet you.

When Tears Fail

*My eyes fail because of tears,
my spirit is greatly troubled;
my heart is poured out on the earth.*
—Lamentations 2:11

*Then David and the people who were with him
raised their voices and wept
until they had no more strength to weep.*
—1 Samuel 30:4

Was there ever a loss or event in your life that left you crushed and crying until there was no strength left to cry another tear? Did the searing sorrow leave your heart shattered in pieces? Were you exhausted under the weight of grief? The Bible records that King David experienced such an event.

We read in 1 Samuel 30 that the Amalekites had carried out an attack on the Negev and on Ziklag, and had overthrown Ziklag and burned it with fire. When King David and his men came to the city, they saw that it was burned with fire, and their wives, their sons, and their daughters had been taken captive. David's two wives, Ahinoam and Abigail, had also been taken. Then David and the people who were with him raised their voices and wept until there was no strength in them to weep. David was in great distress because the people spoke of stoning him, for all the people were embittered because of their sons and daughters being captured.

David strengthened himself in the LORD and then he asked Abiathar, the priest, to bring the ephod, the symbolic garment worn to enter into the holy presence of God. As soon as David received the ephod he inquired of the LORD, saying, *'Shall I pursue this band of raiders? Will I overtake them?'* And God said, *'Pursue, for you will certainly overtake them, and you will certainly rescue everyone.'*

David left with six hundred men. They came to the Besor ravine, where some stayed behind. David and four hundred men continued the pursuit, while two hundred men stayed there, too exhausted to go any further. They found an Egyptian in the countryside and brought him to David. He was given bread and raisin cakes with figs to eat, and water. He ate and regained his strength because he hadn't eaten or drank for three days and nights.

Then David asked him, *'Whose slave are you and where do you come from?'* He told David he was an Egyptian servant boy, the slave of an Amalekite, and that his master abandoned him when he was ill three days earlier. He went on to say, *'We had raided the arid southern plain belonging to the Cherethites,* the territory belonging to Judah, and the southern plain of Caleb. We also burned Ziklag down.'

'Can you guide me to this raiding party?' David asked. The boy responded, 'Make a pledge by God that you won't kill me, or hand me over to my master, and I will guide you to the raiding party.' So the boy led David to them, and he found them scattered all over the countryside, eating, drinking, and celebrating. David attacked them from twilight until evening the next day, killing them all. No one escaped except four hundred young men who fled. David rescued his wives and everything the Amalekites had taken including the sheep and cattle.

King David reached the two hundred men who were exhausted and had stayed behind at the ravine. They and the troops came to greet him. David asked how they were doing. But then all the evil individuals who had accompanied David said, 'We won't share any of the spoil we rescued with them because they didn't go with us. Each of them can take only his wife and children.' David said, 'You shall not do so, my brothers, with what the LORD has given us. He has preserved us and given into our hand the enemy band that came against us.' David divided the supplies equally among the men.

David went from discouragement to potentially facing defeat, but he retrieved all of the belongings, children, and family with the help of an Egyptian servant boy whom God had sent. David extended mercy toward his soldiers who had left him; he knew they were worn down and grief-stricken over their families being taken by the enemy. God's compassion saved David and his camp, as well as the forsaken slave boy.

> *Be strong, and let your heart take courage,*
> *all you who wait for the LORD!*
> —Psalm 31:24

> *Rest in the LORD and wait patiently for Him;*
> *do not get upset because of one*
> *who is successful in his way,*
> *because of the person*
> *who carries out wicked schemes.*
> —Psalm 37:7

David remained quiet with God in prayer and he was vindicated. Only God could have changed the men's hearts toward David and given him victory in the end. He longed for God with his entire being. David found the key to facing the challenges of the day was to seek the LORD at dawn's first appearing and then rest in the LORD'S heart at twilight.

Like David, there will be times when we are alone with no one to comfort or abide empathetically with us. We may find that those we loved and trusted the most have failed to show up and be there for us. When we're feeling parched from not having love, friendship, and encouragement, and are weary like David, we can trust that God is there to soothe and fill the lonely, comfortless places.

If we pause and pray to our Deliverer, He will speak to us through His Word, and the Holy Spirit, to soothe our deep wounds and provide a way out of any trouble. Recalling times when God had helped us before will give us strength for current trials. God came through for us in the past and so will He again. Be assured, God will keep His eyes upon you; He will guide you through everything, knowing what's ahead before you even get there.

> *I will instruct you and teach you*
> *in the way you should go;*
> *I will counsel you with My eye upon you.*
> —Psalm 32:8

> *God, You are my God;*
> *I shall be watching for You;*
> *My soul thirsts for You,*
> *my flesh yearns for You,*
> *In a dry and exhausted land*
> *where there is no water.*
> *When I remember You on my bed,*
> *I meditate on You in the night watches,*
> *For You have been my help,*
> *And in the shadow of Your wings*
> *I sing for joy.*
> *My soul clings to You;*
> *Your right hand takes hold of me.*
> —Psalm 63:1, 6-8

Jesus Christ is our Mediator Who allows us to enter into the holy presence of God. God takes hold of our hand when we delight in His Word. We're all in a weary world and as we grow closer to God with holy desire, we'll find His strength to help us persevere.

The LORD has heard my pleading,
The LORD receives my prayer.
—Psalm 6:9

Let us join our hearts in prayer;
Meeting with our Father on His breast.

Abide With Me

Abide with me: fast falls the eventide;
The darkness deepens; Lord, with me abide.
When other helpers fail and comforts flee,
Help of the helpless, O abide with me.

Swift to its close ebbs out life's little day;
Earth's joys grow dim, its glories pass away.
Change and decay in all around I see.
O thou Who changest not, abide with me.

I need thy presence every passing hour.
What but thy grace can foil the tempter's power?
Who like Thyself my guide and strength can be?
Through cloud and sunshine, O abide with me.

I fear no foe with Thee at hand to bless,
Ills have no weight, and tears no bitterness.
Where is death's sting? Where, grave, thy victory?
I triumph still, if thou abide with me.

Hold thou thy cross before my closing eyes.
Shine through the gloom and point me to the skies.
Heaven's morning breaks and earth's vain shadows flee;
In life, in death, O Lord, abide with me.

—Henry Francis Lyte

I'll Carry You

He does not forget the cry of the needy.
—Psalm 9:12

When a man takes the oath of Knighthood, he pledges to take care of his fellow knights in war, not leaving any man behind. The oath also extends to children and widows of the enemy. Have you considered *leaving no one behind* in regards to those who may need your help? God has laid on the shoulders of the strong to lift up the fallen and carry the fragile until they are made whole.

Learn to do good; seek justice,
rebuke the oppressor,
obtain justice for the orphan,
plead for the widow's case.
—Isaiah 1:17

Orphans lack experience and protectors; parents who love them unconditionally and defend them. Without a bonded family, they can fall prey to oppression. It's therefore urgent that we befriend, defend, and do justice for the fatherless and the orphans. Widows and orphans have an extra measure of grace, and since God deems this necessary, so should we.

> *Pure and undefiled religion in*
> *the sight of our God and Father is this:*
> *to visit orphans and widows in their distress,*
> *and to keep oneself unstained by the world.*
> *—James 1:27*

True religion supports and visits those in distress; they watch over, befriend, and meet their physcial, emotional, and spiritual needs. Orphans and widows are deserving of the highest level of charity and mercy. When we listen and speak to their heart, while sympathizing in their distresses, we are encouraging orphans and widows with God's eternal love.

Jesus Christ left us an example of perfect love that defends, protects, and stands with the lonely and outcast of society. If we are to have pure religion and imitate God, we are to be a helper to the fatherless as seen in James 1:27. Hosea reads: *For in You the orphan finds mercy.* Benevolent souls who pity and give to those in need will also find comfort and prosperity for burdens that come in their life.

> *And if you offer yourself to the hungry*
> *and satisfy the need of the afflicted,*
> *then your light will rise in darkness,*
> *and your gloom will become like midday.*
> *—Isaiah 58:10*

If you've been forced to live far from the comforts of a loving home, and perhaps shuffled among strangers, Christ is a rock of serenity for you to hold on to. He will calm your overwhelmed heart with peace and love that exceeds any human touch. God is your supreme refuge from all that has harmed and hurt you. Open the Word and hide in the all-encompassing heart of God.

Be their shepherd and carry them forever.
—Psalm 28:9

Just as the eagle broods over her young to impart warmth and vitality, God influences us with His Spirit to inspire and strengthen. Eagles demonstrate extraordinary affection for their young especially when they carry them on their backs after the little ones become weary of flying. God will hold onto us and never let us go no matter what trial or storm blows our way.

*As an eagle stirs up its nest,
And hovers over its young,
He spread His wings, He caught them,
He carried them on His pinions.*
—Deuteronomy 32:11

Moses penned the words above at the end of his life. Does it not amaze you that Moses, a beloved servant of God, used such a tender example to portray God's devoted heart for His own? Scripture records that God buried him and no one knows where his grave is. We all want to be cherished that deeply, don't we? If we honor and love God, we are promised the depth of love Moses experienced with Him. He will carry us when we are weary. And when our time on earth is ended, God will also take us up, folded forever in His breast.

> *And He buried him (Moses) in the valley in the land*
> *of Moab, opposite Beth-peor;*
> *but no one knows his burial place to this day.*
> *—Deuteronomy 34:6*

Whether we've been orphans at birth or made orphans later when our natural parents have died, God has been there and will ever be there to gather and hold us close to His bosom. We can desire, with great anticipation, that we'll be held forever in the arms of our Eternal Friend and Father—our everlasting blood family.

> *For my father and my mother have forsaken me,*
> *but the LORD will take me up.*
> *—Psalm 27:10*

God Will Take Care of You

Be not dismayed whate'er betide,
God will take care of you;
Beneath his wings of love abide,
God will take care of you.

Refrain:
God will take care of you,
Through ev'ry day, o'er all the way;
He will take care of you,
God will take care of you.

Through days of toil when heart doth fail,
God will take care of you;
When dangers fierce your path assail,
God will take care of you. [Refrain]

No matter what may be the test,
God will take care of you;
Lean, weary one, upon his breast,
God will take care of you. [Refrain]

—Civilla D. Martin

Crushed and Broken

Touched by a loving heart, wakened by kindness,
Chords that were broken will vibrate once more.
—Fanny J. Crosby

Whoever sings songs to a heavy heart
is like one who takes off a
garment on a cold day,
and like vinegar on soda.
—Proverbs 25:20

The Scripture above packs a huge message to those of us who may have no idea what it's like to suffer with a heavy heart, or a mental collapse. We're advised that it's not only inappropriate and cruel to sing songs to a heavy heart, but counter-productive because it often makes matters worse.

When an individual is sad and his pain is acknowledged, the suffering soul will begin to experience hope through the other's genuine love and concern. While there is a severe and deep depression that needs to be addressed professionally, in many cases, doses of God's extravagant love and spiritual encouragement help to set the brokenhearted on the path to healing. Our LORD Jesus Christ was described as One Who was acquainted with grief. He is our example of perfect love and tenderness toward the brokenhearted.

We who are strong can be friends of sympathy and understanding to the crushed. Christ's perfect example of One Who always acted out of consideration for others, no matter what it cost Him, is our guide to helping others with extraordinary love. We don't want to be the cause of others feeling rejection and hurt, but sometimes we are without being aware of it. Phrases—*count your blessings, it could be worse, you're not the only one suffering, cheer up, be positive, it's time to move on, stop dwelling on it*—can also drive one's pain further inward. Responses like these are why many don't trust others with their inner sorrows and struggles; they just can't handle another rejection placed upon their already fragile spirit. This is sad and has at times been the final blow to an already depressed, lonely, and rejected individual.

The mouth of a righteous man is a well of life.
—Proverbs 10:11

When the fragile are treated with compassion, acceptance, and without judgment, or minimizing their circumstances, it's possible to save another from making a permanent, life-altering solution for a transient and solvable problem. The hurt need to know they are valued and have help with their burdens. We must be sensitive to their pain even if we don't understand it. Allowing others their own pace to work through difficulties and being an attentive presence is sometimes the best support we can give and the best friend we can be.

Embrace the lonely and discouraged,
Be their well of hope and understanding.

For You light my lamp;
The LORD my God illumines my darkness.
—Psalm 18:28

God will ignite our darkness with His pleading candle—the hope of Christ—if we allow Him. Our sorrowful heart will be revived and comforted when He picks us up and carries us away from a melancholy, hopeless, and despairing existence.

The enemy wants us to fall into despair and give in to dark thoughts so that they can take root and eventually take us out. He does this by trying to convince us that others would be better off without us, no one would miss us, or care if we died. But those are lies and are not of God. There's always someone who loves us even if we don't believe it. Often we are more loved and cherished than we realize. A great example of this is seen in George Bailey, a fictional character in the film, *It's a Wonderful Life*.

George Bailey was a charitable individual who had spent his life giving to the people of Bedford Falls. It was Christmas Eve, as the film opened, and George considered himself a failure, facing financial ruin and arrest over the shortage of $8000.00. The money was believed to have been lost, but was stolen by Mr. Potter, the wealthiest and meanest man in Bedford Falls. George lost hope and decided to take his life by jumping over a bridge. Before he had a chance to leap into the bitter, freezing water, however, an angel (Clarence) came to rescue him. Clarence allowed George to see what life for the residents of Bedford Falls would have been like had he never been born.

The angel helped George to relive the multitude of selfless acts he had performed. He saw that his younger brother would have died had he not been there to save him from drowning. A grieving druggist would have delivered poison by mistake to an ailing child if George had not intervened, taking a beating for it. If he had not been alive to forgo college and a long-planned trip to Europe, he would have let down depression-era customers at the Bailey Building and Loan. And Mr. Potter would have taken over Bedford Mills and reduced its inhabitants to penury.

Clarence took George through a nightmarish odyssey where Bedford Falls was Pottersville slum, wherein none of his friends or family recognized him. Fortunately George cried out, '*I want to live again* . . . *I want to live again*', after realizing how he had touched and helped so many people. His spirit was revived after returning home. Friends, acquaintances, and family came to his house and gave him money, support, and love after they had heard about his troubles and the threats of jail.

We see from this touching story that George Bailey lost sight of his purpose and value when troubles came looming. He thought he was alone and saw no way out; discouragement had blurred his vision of what was really true. He thought suicide was a way out of the unbearable pain. George Bailey didn't want to die; he wanted relief from the burdens of his life.

Imagine the rescue, love, and support of family and friends denied George if he had leapt from the bridge on that despairing Christmas Eve. Additionally, imagine the gut-wrenching sorrow he would have left behind for his impressionable children, devoted wife, and loving brother. This is why it's urgent that we stay focused with an intentional pursuit to seek the LORD'S face in prayer, engage His Word for support and guidance, and reach out to friends and loved ones when life is difficult.

We can all have moments like George Bailey when we, too, lose hope or fail to see a way out of our adversities. God sends angels, friends, family, and sometimes people we don't know to rally around and help us. We need to give people a chance to know our struggles so that we are able, through them, to see the beauty inside ourselves. When we allow the LORD time to intervene, we begin to see the unique assets we possess.

*The LORD also will be a refuge for the oppressed,
a refuge in times of trouble.*
—Psalm 9:9

If we allow the same thoughts to take hold day in and day out, we fail to release ourselves from a perpetual prison of hopelessness and despair. We can overcome these feelings if we keep reaching forward with a vision of how we want our life to be. It may be helpful to record or make a visual collage of our aspirations in that hope-filled future. Once we've identified our goals, it can be beneficial to list the steps needed to accomplish them.

Choosing to take small steps each day is a more reasonable and realistic way to go about achieving success. To some, this may seem like a daunting task when just getting through a day is all one can manage. What's important is that we're getting there, even if it is tiny steps and a few setbacks along the way. In doing this, we begin to let go of the past—the unchangeable past we all have—that serves only to steal our joy, peace, and personal growth if we keep returning to it as the definer of ourselves, our relationships, and our world.

Often rooted in severe depression are feelings of shame, stress, anger, and discontentment. It's important for the suffering soul to define whether the feelings align with God's heart. Christ's blood on the cross saves us from everything, including fleeting and fluctuating feelings and thoughts. If there's something we've done that has been the cause of us feeling bad, then confessing that to God and asking for help is a way to heal the nagging feeling of shame. We are more than our wounded past and our failures. If we hold firmly to God and wait for His rescue, there's absolutely nothing that can prevent God's goodness.

Our moods influence us daily, so it's important to not allow our moods or feelings to rule over sound reasoning. We must take charge of them, as well as repetitive thoughts that can sabotage our lives. Wisdom obtained in 2 Corinthians 10:5 says that God desires we take captive our thoughts. It is possible to choose what we dwell on and what we allow as focus in our lives. Further, what we focus on becomes our life's reality. Our thoughts are powerful and either lift up or depress and discourage us.

Anger can be a very detrimental emotion if allowed to go unchecked. Each night before we go to bed, it would be wise to forgive those who have wronged us and to let go of hate-filled thoughts. When anger is allowed to fester overnight and for days upon days, it can soon become a cancer that destroys a tranquil mind.

Sometimes expectations we have of ourselves, or of others, can fuel depression. It can help to not set unrealistic expectations. Having broad thinking with a broad scope of solutions and possibilities allows our mind to make allowances for ourselves and others. Because someone may not return our call or respond to our email at a specific time, for example, doesn't necessary mean they have forgotten us, don't want to talk to us, or worse, have cut us out of their lives. It could simply mean they, too, have a lot going on and are planning to respond at a more opportune time. We'd all be wise to learn the art of separating our feelings and beliefs from the facts before rushing to judgment or action.

Depression and disappointments can distort our reality, thereby making it difficult for us to see the beautiful attributes we possess, and the importance of who we are and are to become. This is a good time to enlist help from your family, friends, co-workers, classmates, etc. This idea requires a bag, small box, or a container with a lid. You may wish to contact those you associate with, or have close ties, and tell them how you're feeling. You need only to express what you feel comfortable disclosing and then ask if each would share a song, a prayer, a poem, Scripture, or personal words of encouragement to help you. Have each one add the tokens to the box or bag. Then on difficult days, take out a few and read them. You'd be surprised at how helpful this is. Our family and friends would want to be a part of helping us if they knew we were struggling and feeling down. Expressions like this can help to remind us of our value among those who love us.

It can be helpful to gather Scripture, songs, and inspiring quotes to keep nearby—in your car, in your home, on a mirror, in a pocket, a purse, or a journal—and reflect on those when sadness or hopelessness consumes your spirit. Have a trusted friend's contact information on hand at all times. Consider these tokens of encouragement as a *first aid kit* to help alleviate darkness and despair. Be ready, at all times, to invite the Light of hope to lift you out of any unexpected crisis.

> *His radiance is like the sunlight;*
> *He has rays flashing from His hand,*
> *And the hiding of His might is there.*
> —Habakkuk 3:4

Some stress is unavoidable, but if you are experiencing an overload of stress, it can be helpful to evaluate your life and see where you can reduce stressors. It may mean that you hang out with different friends, look for another job, or clean up your life from negativity. This would also be a good time to take some time out, perhaps plan an uplifting event to soothe ravaged nerves.

Evaluating what we eat and drink throughout the day may be helpful in pinpointing a trigger for shifting moods and restless sleep. Sleep deprivation can lead to bouts of depression. Perhaps limit caffeine before bedtime and focus your diet on foods that help to promote balanced nutrition for both mind and body. A diet rich with vegetables, fruits, fish, proteins, grains, and healthy fats can be a great defense against depression.

Getting off the sofa and taking a walk or getting some other form of exercise can help your body produce endorphins, those good-feeling hormones in your brain that energize your spirits. Exercise promotes changes in the brain, such as neural growth, reduced inflammation, and new activity patterns that promote feelings of calm and well-being. It also increases energy throughout the day, better sleep at night, improved memory, and boosting overall mood while relaxing the mind. Studies show that even a 10 minute brisk walk can help treat mild to moderate depression and anxiety. Maintaining an exercise schedule can also help to prevent a relapse. Taking a few strolls in nature serves as a distraction, allowing quiet reflection away from what's troubling the mind and heart.

> *We have to tie our spiritual laces*
> *And keep moving forward,*
> *As we see the past disappearing*
> *In the rear-view mirror.*

Soaking in a few minutes of sunlight can also help to soothe despair and anxiety. Why not ask a few friends to meet you at a park for a 'friendship walk' or just to sit and have a picnic on a warm sunny day? Even if you can't meet with friends every day, just having an emotional support group, with those you already know and trust, can do wonders for your spirit. This time can also allow an avenue for you to trust others with what's going on in your life. Often we find that others feel as we do; they just haven't told us yet.

It's possible to dial up a low spirit with positive energy. Because our world tends to be doom and gloom and focusing on something negative creeping around every corner, we'd all be happier for moments where we made laughter an essential part of our daily lives. The research on laughter tells us it improves immune function, lowers stress, and like exercise, releases endorphins.

Laughter can be one of the best sedatives in our holistic apothecary. Studies indicate that laughter can stimulate the immune system and organs, increase oxygen to the cells, relieve stress on the heart and help to reduce blood pressure, nervous tension, and pain while improving moods. If we are able to laugh more and encourage others to laugh with us, we not only lift up ourselves, but those around us. I like to term this as 'buddy bonding laughter' where there's emotional bonding of friendship, inspiration, and support. Inspiring others and ourselves to laugh can be addictive, and isn't that the best kind of addictive behavior? We're all attracted to feeling better and having our spirit soothed and nurtured.

One of the most effective ways to incorporate laughter in our lives is to engage with others who are witty and enjoyable. If you're one who suffers with a discouraged, depressed spirit, gather a few of the most positive people you know and plan a clean, fun party or event. And just be yourself—goofy, charismatic, and authentic—allowing others to see that the person who's buried within is a unique soul with much to share. Laughter can be a great balm of healing.

God has the power to chase away
The gloomy clouds hovering over our world;
Through others, He will fill the atmosphere with joy.

It can be helpful to remember our blessings when we're feeling heavy in heart. Consider making a list of what you're grateful for and looking at it when you're in a dark place. Even if those things don't seem true at the time, keep reminding yourself of them, saying out loud, *It's going to be okay because I have so much to live for, despite not realizing it at this very moment.* Shifting our mindset to one of praise and thanksgiving can be great medicine for a loathing spirit. Additionally, when we shift the focus away from ourselves to helping others, we find a respite from our own woes. When we are proactive in what's allowed on our emotional and mental radar, we can then weed out potential threats and begin the road to recovery.

Reminding ourselves of the incredible insight and heightened joy that comes at the end of suffering gives us strength. Joy emerges after the season of sorrow has passed. Consider reading Job's tragic story in the Bible and remind yourself that just as God guided Job through his troubles, He'll do the same for you. Fall in God's outstretched arms and let Him carry you too. The changing seasons tell us that valleys come and they go; so hold on, and soon you'll have climbed that mountain with God's help.

It may not be easy, and a struggle each time to do the suggestions mentioned previously, but you will feel so much better at the end of the day. And as you develop good proactive habits, each new dawn will become brighter and brighter until the dark night has faded.

Why are you in despair, my soul?
And why are you restless within me?
Wait for God, for I will again praise Him
For the help of His presence, my God.
—Psalm 42:5

Dearest, awesome, Father,
Please cast Your favor on my life;
Make all the dark shadows flee
And surround me in Your healing Light.

Often an underlining component of a cast down spirit is a childhood where validation and unconditional love were not met. If you've never had those affirmations, God offers them to you now and forever. He says to you: *I love you, you're valuable to Me, I cherish you, I'll protect you and keep you safe, I'll be kind to you, I'll help you through this, I'll never leave nor forsake you, you belong to Me and always will.* As God holds you, He regards you as a jeweled crown of exceeding beauty and glory. You are no longer forsaken and desolate; He calls you His Delight!

You shall be a crown of beauty
in the hand of the LORD,
and a royal diadem in the hand of your God.
It will no longer be said to you, 'Forsaken,'
Nor to your land will it
any longer be said, 'Desolate';
But you will be called, 'My delight is in her,'
And your land, 'Married';
For the LORD delights in you,
And to Him your land will be married.
—Isaiah 62:3-4

From the end of the earth will I cry unto thee,
when my heart is overwhelmed,
lead me to the rock that is higher than I.
—Psalm 61:2

If you observe changes in a friend or family member, don't be afraid to ask them if they are okay, if they are thinking of hurting themselves, or if they would like to talk about what's bothering them. Check on them frequently and consider becoming their faithful *followup-buddy* who has made a commitment to call, text, email, or drop by their home if they have not been heard from by a designated check-in time. Give them a big hug even if you can do nothing more. Be that one person they can trust and allow them to share their pain, without judgment or advice, because you could be cutting it in half, if not totally eliminating it by doing so. Through your compassion, they regain strength, resolve, and hope is ignited within.

Many who have survived a suicide attempt later said they were relieved they had failed at taking their lives. The passage of time allowed the survivors to settle their minds, get help, and gather more insight about themselves and the circumstances that drove them to wanting to end their lives. They also realized they were loved by many friends and family, but the dark despair had prevented those *loving thoughts* at the time of their dire need. Others expressed they had experienced a moment of intense anger that drove them to attempt suicide, only to find later their anger, like many emotions, was fleeting and unreliable.

> *There are in each the seeds of a heroic ardor,*
> *Which need only to be stirred in*
> *With the soil where they lie.*
> *I don't want to feel as if my life*
> *Were a sojourn any longer.*
> *It is time now that I begin to live.*
> *—Henry David Thoreau*

For those of us who have lost a loved one or close friend to suicide, we are left with incredible pain and questions that will plague us throughout our lives. Even if we were kind, nurturing, and not the cause of our loved one choosing to die, many of us still blame ourselves and wonder what we could have done differently. We try to trace the horrendous and desperate path their mind took when it could no longer endure to the next heartbeat, only to find a perpetual cycle of sorrow leading nowhere. Grief is complicated enough, but combined with loss that's traumatic, violent, and senseless, it can leave the heart scarred without a sense of closure.

> *You can't tell your heart not to break when it's lost*
> *some of the most beloved you've ever known.*

How do we face tomorrow when the ones we love the deepest aren't here with us to greet the next sunrise? Leaving the unrelenting questions with the LORD will help to free our souls from some of the pain we're left with when we've lost a dear one to suicide. Only God has the answers and only He knows the heart and how it has suffered. Accepting that God knows and loves on a level our finite minds cannot comprehend is a place to begin when we grapple with suicide's devastating aftermath. Some wounds may never heal on this side of Heaven; all we can do is to keep pressing into the breast of God until Eternity restores the fractures of our lives.

> *Even to your old age I will be the same,*
> *And even to your graying years I will carry you!*
> *I have done it, and I will bear you;*
> *And I will carry you and I will save you.*
> —Isaiah 46:4

> *And of Benjamin he said, 'The beloved of the LORD*
> *shall dwell in safety by him; and the LORD shall*
> *cover him all the day long, and he shall dwell*
> *between His shoulders.'*
> —Deuteronomy 33:12

> *The heart knows its own bitterness,*
> *And a stranger does not share its joy.*
> —Proverbs 14:10

We are reminded in the above Scripture that all are alone when it comes to being fully known and understood by another. But not so when it comes to God; He's known us before our conception. There are sacred places within all of us that only God can relieve and restore.

> *Before I formed you in the womb I knew you,*
> *And before you were born I consecrated you.*
> *—Jeremiah 1:5*

> *Because He has inclined His Ear to me,*
> *therefore I will call upon Him as long as I live.*
> *—Psalm 116:2*

When we are too weak to speak and sobbing on our pillows, the LORD'S heart lays beside us to receive every word of our prayer. From the Courts of Heaven, God is hearing your deep prayers. Keep pouring out your heart to Him and keep holding on to your faith.

> *Cover yourself in blankets of prayer*
> *And God's arms of hope will embrace you*
> *When you're afraid and in despair.*
> *Run to the nail-scarred hands*
> *Of your Advocate, Jesus our Savior;*
> *He's been there through it all*
> *And has seen the tearful, thorny path*
> *Your heart has taken.*

If you're struggling and feeling hopeless, give God a chance to speak life to you. Place your trust in your amazing Father. Fight those moments with prayer and God's Word. Allow yourself to be vulnerable to someone, such as a doctor, family member, friend, minister, or an elder. Consider joining a support group or calling a crisis hotline where there is shared understanding and mutual empathy. Dark days don't last forever even though dark moments or seasons can seem like a perpetual moment, one coming upon another. Ride through the darkness because you can get to the other side if you reach out to even one person and trust him or her to help you.

Making drastic decisions while you are depressed is not in your best interest. Before taking life-altering measures to alleviate a momentary problem, choose to live through the despair; life-saving light will come and the day will turn around if you give it time. God can transform your heart and give a place to all that you've gone through. Even your deepest regrets will benefit your future if you surrender your heart to God. Remember you are a one and only design and your life has a purpose.

Each time dark thoughts—*no one will miss me, no one loves me, I'm undeserving of love and forgiveness because I've messed up beyond repair, everyone's better off without me, why live another day when every day is hopeless*—come to mind, choose life-giving words instead. Repeat to yourself: *My family, especially my parents, will grieve and I'll leave them with insurmountable anguish for the rest of their lives if I take my life. No one's better off without me because I'm unique and made for a plan that only God has called me to fulfill. God forgives my wrongs because I've repented and turned away from sin and am determined to do my best. Jesus died on the cross for me; God's grace, mercy, and love is reaching down and will rescue me, I just need to be still and wait on Him.* What Satan intends for harm, God intends for good . . . stay to see the end that God has planned for you, you don't want to miss it!

> As for you, you meant evil against me,
> but God meant it for good
> in order to bring about this present result,
> to keep many people alive.
> —Genesis 50:20

> For I am convinced that neither death,
> nor life, nor angels,
> nor principalities, nor things present,
> nor things to come,
> nor powers, nor height, nor depth,
> nor any other created thing
> will be able to separate us from the love of God
> hat is in Christ Jesus our LORD.
> —Romans 8:38-39

All depression should be taken seriously. Be encouraged, the LORD'S empathetic heart is vast and open to you. He feels deepest sorrow for you; deeper than a mother's love is God's tender affection for you. He longs to soothe the ache, settle internal torments of feeling unworthy of love, forgiveness, and value. He desires to hold you close to His breast and set you on the path of light where restoration can begin. He longs to instill hope—His hope—that's not dependent upon how you feel, your circumstances, or what you have accomplished, but is based upon the One Who has promised to never leave nor forsake you.

If you're in a broken place, know that Jesus is kneeling beside you, He's waiting to scoop you up into His arms. Let Him have the baggage, and never look back; you don't belong there. Leave the wreckage behind and choose God, He has a future for you, trust Him. God's power can break through any blurry dark path; there's no mess too big for Him to mop up. Even if some bridges have been burned to the ground, He can build new ones for you to step onto with newfound strength. Sob on God's shoulder, cry to Him endlessly—whatever you need to do—as you go through the storm, because nothing you experience will return void when God's the pilot of your life.

God never promised to remove the valleys of pain and sorrow from our lives, but He did promise to carry us through them. Take hold of His timeless Light and let Him lead you out of the spirit of despair. Allow Him be the mirror reflecting your soul where you'll be redefined by a higher calling that heals and transforms.

In the darkest places of our lives,
God's a candle to lead us out.

Whispering Hope

Soft as the voice of an angel,
Breathing a lesson unheard,
Hope with a gentle persuasion
Whispers her comforting word:
Wait till the darkness is over,
Wait till the tempest is done,
Hope for the sunshine tomorrow,
After the shower is gone.

Refrain:
Whispering hope, oh, how welcome thy voice,
Making my heart in its sorrow rejoice.

If, in the dusk of the twilight,
Dim be the region afar,
Will not the deepening darkness
Brighten the glimmering star?
Then when the night is upon us,
Why should the heart sink away?
When the dark midnight is over,
Watch for the breaking of day. [Refrain]

Hope, as an anchor so steadfast,
Rends the dark veil for the soul,
Whither the Master has entered,
Robbing the grave of its goal;
Come then, oh come, glad fruition,
Come to my sad weary heart;
Come, O Thou blest hope of glory,
Never, oh, never depart. [Refrain]

—Septimus Winner

Beautiful Evergreen

*To grant those who mourn in Zion,
giving them a garland instead of ashes,
the oil of gladness instead of mourning,
the cloak of praise instead of a disheartened spirit.
So they will be called oaks of righteousness,
the planting of the LORD, that He may be glorified.*
—Isaiah 61:3

The Bible teaches us that it was tradition for Jews to put on sackcloth and spread dust and ashes on their heads in times of mourning. We, too, will encounter times of tears. The Messiah didn't come as a Savior for only the Jews, but for all people.

God has promised, through His son, beauty—a beautiful crown, or garland—in place of our sorrow. We can face our grief knowing that with God, we'll find the strength needed to cope and survive. When God comforts, our heavy spirits will be lifted in praise of Him. This is why we may encounter a Christian who's stable and steady in their faith, yet suffering profoundly. As we grow in God, we become more resistant to a disheartened spirit. It may take some us all of our lives to reach this kind of spiritual stability, but isn't it worth every effort to try and have it now?

When God created the world He spoke trees into existence. We find throughout Scripture that trees were often symbols of poetry and used as metaphors. The average life span of an oak tree is 200 to 300 years and some varieties, with proper conditions, can grow well over 100 feet tall. Most oaks are deciduous, but some are evergreen.

The oak tree supplies the needs of several of God's creatures. Many animals and insects eat the acorns and the leaves. Some forms of wildlife use the bark and twigs to build their nests. Small animals, mammals, and larger animals use the branches, and the oak's canopy of leaves for shade and protection. God's thoughtfulness to protect and provide for His creation is awesome and beautiful. His extravagant beauty also extends to us as found in Isaiah 61:3. His righteous children are as oak trees—lofty, strong, and magnificent.

When our lives have been torn down, God can rebuild us to remain immortal. And as we live for God, our roots grow deeper and firmer in Him. Because of His protective love, we stand taller and even more resistant to sin, and resilient to the changing cruel weather of our human existence. Almighty God is our umbrella of refuge when the rains of sorrow pour and the stormy seasons of adversity crush our hearts.

> *The fear of the LORD is a fountain of life,*
> *By which one may avoid the snares of death.*
> *—Proverbs 14:27*

> *I will be like the dew to Israel;*
> *He will blossom like the lily,*
> *And he will take root like the cedars of Lebanon.*
> *—Hosea 14:5*

The scripture above is a beautiful metaphor of God's care. He will refresh all with spiritual blessings, day to day, as He did for the people of Israel. He is to our soul a lily of pure beauty. In Him, we are deeply rooted with strength and will remain strong, even in the gloom of winter. And like the cedar tree with its lovely outstretched arms, God will provide grace and protection for our souls.

> *And the LORD will continually guide you,*
> *and satisfy your desire in scorched places,*
> *and give strength to your bones;*
> *And you will be like a watered garden,*
> *and like a spring of water whose waters do not fail.*
> *—Isaiah 58:11*

We must step into God's presence to receive blessings and protection. The LORD will go before us and lead us with strength when we are weary and our burdens are heavier than we can bear. He will shower refreshing rain on the parched places of our lives. We will be like a paradise garden, lush and vibrant; its spring will flow with pardon, peace, and joy, ever open and abundant.

> *Having been firmly rooted*
> *and now being built up in Him*
> *and established in your faith,*
> *just as you were instructed,*
> *and overflowing with gratitude.*
> *—Colossians 2:7*

A faithful life, grounded in truth, glorifies God in all of His splendor. He will cure our wounds, comfort us in our sorrow, and release us from the bondage of an oppressed spirit when we are planted in His House. Like oak trees, we will flourish in the Courts of our God and will never be forgotten.

> *Surely he shall not be moved forever:*
> *the righteous shall be in everlasting remembrance.*
> *—Psalm 12:6*

> *Blessed is the man who trusts in the LORD,*
> *whose trust is the LORD.*
> *He is like a tree planted by water,*
> *that sends out its roots by the stream,*
> *and does not fear when heat comes,*
> *for its leaves remain green,*
> *and is not anxious in the year of drought,*
> *for it does not cease to bear fruit.*
> *—Jeremiah 17:7-8*

Wings

*For whoever has despised
the day of small things shall rejoice,
and shall see the plumb line
in the hand of Zerubbabel.*
—Zechariah 4:10

Zechariah was engaged in the building of the temple and when its foundations were laid, others thought it was small. God admonishes all of us not to despise or have contempt for small beginnings. He accepts the efforts of the feeble and frail and encourages the weak believers. The next time we see someone attempting to achieve a goal, yet struggling with a small or seemingly insignificant beginning, we should do whatever we can to inspire their progress. Let's remember we, too, were once weak and God had compassion for us.

God's strength is perfected in weakness. The Bible is full of examples where God's power helped the small. God saved Joseph from prison, David from the sheepfold, Daniel from slavery, and Rahab after she had welcomed the spies in peace. God sent Jesus as a carpenter to die on the cross, thereby saving the world. If we want to be great, we must esteem God as the Great I Am.

Encouragement gives the spirit wings.

Have your wings been clipped before you even had a chance to fly and now you don't have the strength to give it another try? Has there been a time in your life when you felt small and insignificant? Has someone despised your small beginning and left you tattered and torn? Forgive them and let God carry you on His shoulders and He'll give you new wings—wings with imperial power—to soar like an eagle, above it all.

He restores my soul.
He leads me in paths of righteousness
for his name's sake.
—Psalm 23:3

David trusted that God would strengthen and renew his soul as noted in the Scripture above. And even though our lives may not have turned out as we had hoped, we can still trust that God will restore our weary and depleted spirits. In time, we'll enjoy lush green meadows while walking hand in hand with our LORD along the lovely shores of hope. The Bible is full of Scripture that reassures that if we remain committed and true to God's heart, not only will our life be restored, but our entire being, spirit and soul. He is the Fire that ignites our life, both physically and eternally!

You may feel weak without energy or ambition to realize your goals or strive for the best you can be. The truth is, we're all weak in comparison to Deity—whether we're in the depths of despair and brokenness, or enjoying a season of refreshing and accomplishment—God is still greater and we are still weak. We need God to be our pilot no matter who we are, what we have achieved, how we feel about ourselves, or what others may think of us.

Look through the lens of Christ
And you'll see your beautiful potential.

Dimly Burning

*God's not after perfection,
He's after our heart.*

*A bent reed He will not break off,
and a dimly burning wick He will not extinguish,
until He leads justice to victory.
And in His name the Gentiles will hope.
—Matthew 12:20-21*

Jesus Christ is our hope and trust. He was affectionate to the broken, lonely, and outcast who came into His presence. His approachable personality, and tender compassionate ways touched and changed hearts.

Christ sought those who were, perhaps by others' standards, fragile and pathetic. Jesus did not view the lowly this way, but instead carried them gently in His arms while bestowing them with spiritual affection. Even if they had little strength—emotionally, spiritually, physically, and on the verge of giving up—Christ stood by them, perhaps when no one else would, demonstrating His love and commitment to them.

Christ's disciples also struggled in their faith, but Jesus did not discourage, reject, or cast them out. No, on the contrary, He loved them deeply and affectionately, considering them as *family*. And so it will be with us who surrender all that we are to Him, even if all we are is weak and small. He reassures the bruised reed he will not be broken, or trodden down, but supported and made stronger. The believer whose faith is dimly lit and smoking with no flame, Christ will not blow out.

Early in our faith, many of us are bruised reeds and dimly burning candles, yet Jesus Christ has mercy. Just as He was patient with us when we were beginners in the faith, so must we be with others who are fragile and young. When we live an example of God's love and mercy toward others, they can't help but fall in love with Him. We extend God's love by being the hand of love that helps them up when they've fallen or helps to carry them when the burdens of life become too great. These benevolent acts are a spark to a spirit that's barely hanging on.

We're all going to be weak at times even when we've loved and honored God for many years. God accepts a heart willing to take yet another step despite feeling he's unworthy, feeble, wobbly, and on the verge of burning out. To find healing and strength, we must study Christ's pure example and try to emulate His approachable presence. We owe God our lives for sending His son to defend and fight for us.

Nothing is incurable for our Awesome God. He wraps His arms around us and fills the lonely places with His mercy and salvation. He encourages sincerity, though we may have great infirmity. He recognizes we won't be sinless, but accepts a meek and humble heart.

Some in today's world consider humility a weakness, but that's not true. Humility is strength shrouded in temperance and self control. God's grace, given through His son on the cross, can dissolve any flaw when the soul is allowed to grow under the affirming Light of Eternity. Small seeds of faith will bloom and blossom when nourished with encouragement.

Words and Thoughts

*Pleasant words are a honeycomb,
sweet to the soul and healing to the bones.*
—Proverbs 16:24

*I was mute and silent;
I held my peace to no avail,
and my distress grew worse.
My heart became hot within me.
As I mused, the fire burned;
then I spoke with my tongue.*
—Psalm 39:2

The psalmist kept his thoughts to himself, choosing not to speak even one word of good or bad. David didn't defend himself, or express vindication of any kind. But in choosing to bury his thoughts, he was met with further harm and anguish of heart. The suppressive brooding increased his trouble and ultimately was not conducive to a balanced and tranquil mind. Upon reflection, David came to understand that this method of dealing with his life was not wise. Just like David, many good men and women have attempted to do the same, thinking that this would help alleviate agonies that can often weigh down a heart.

Whether our thoughts are good or bad, our circumstances pure or evil, we are never called to suppress them within, thereby cutting off all communication with God or others, and then hope to feel better later. God calls us to express our heart to Him; the One Who can restore, affirm, and convict if necessary. Our communication with God should be deep and expansive with total transparency. When we pour out the contents of our heart to God, we can count on the answers we're seeking, and the relief we're needing. God has us covered and guarded.

> *When I kept silent about my sin,*
> *my body wasted away*
> *through my groaning all day long.*
> —Psalm 32:3

There is a balance to what we should share with others. We don't have permission to reveal every thought that arises in our mind. Some may argue that if something is true about another then it's okay to repeat. Discretion begs the merciful soul to ponder before speaking ill of others or sharing others' personal information. It's a privilege to take our thoughts and worries to God. And it's an honor when someone entrusts us with their troubles and secrets. But prayer requests are never to be an excuse to talk and gossip about others. We don't have the right to reveal others' confidences when we've been asked to pray for another. A person of integrity will not disclose the names or the contents, but will simply ask for prayers in secret. Since words cannot be taken back, we are wise to give serious consideration to the words we speak.

> *One who guards his mouth protects his life;*
> *one who opens wide his lips comes to ruin.*
> *—Proverbs 13:3*

Most of us can say we have said things that have crushed the spirit of another. And there have been times when others have felt healed, encouraged, and comforted by our treatment of them.

> *There is one who speaks rashly*
> *like the thrusts of a sword,*
> *but the tongue of the wise brings healing.*
> *—Proverbs 12:18*

> *A soothing tongue is a tree of life,*
> *but perversion in it crushes the spirit.*
> *—Proverbs 15:4*

For as long as we live in our mortal bodies, we will be in an ongoing battle to train our tongues for wholesome and uplifting dialogue. Let's decide today to speak life, hope, love, and healing words of affirmation, to not only our own soul, but to all we're blessed meeting.

> *A person has joy in an apt answer,*
> *and how delightful is a timely word!*
> *—Proverbs 15:23*

Scared of the Spider

If you believe, then nothing can bring you down.
When it's God's will, then nothing will stop you.

His radiance is like the sunlight.
—Habakkuk 3:4

Most of us experience fear and doubt during seasons of our lives. Fear can be paralyzing and sometimes unfounded; at other times, understandably expected. I recall when my son was four years of age and we were visiting some friends who lived nearby. While at their house we were in their dark cellar, discussing their pipes and potential trouble brewing. Suddenly a spider appeared and my son shuddered in fear. While I sought to comfort him, our friend's husband blurted, *'You're not scared of a little ole spider are you? He won't hurt you, you're so much bigger than he is!'* I looked at the man and said, *'But you're not the one scared of the spider!'* He chuckled with nothing left to say.

Have you ever been afraid and it seemed no one understood or they trivialized your feelings? I recall one stormy evening when I was in foster care. I was lying in my bed and could hear the thunder clap and see the lightning running through the sky as I peered out the window beside my bed. I quickly threw the cover over my head, in an attempt to hide from the scary storm, and avoid being struck by lightning. My foster mother walked in the room and said, *'You can't hide from God!'* I quickly uncovered my head and thought about the words she had said. *But I'm not afraid of God,* I thought, *why did she say that?* I was merely afraid of the storm. If she had just sat beside my bed, reassuring me that God was with me, and that the storm would pass, my nerves would have settled.

We find in the example of Peter walking on water (Matthew 14) that when we call to the LORD, He will stretch out His arm and save us. The LORD bade for the apostle to come to Him on the water and Peter trusted and went to His LORD. Peter saw his own frailty and weakness in the midst of God's great abiding presence.

The LORD allows us the choice to surrender and trust or to go our own way and drown in fears. When we take our focus away from Christ and place it on the magnitude of our difficulties, we begin to fall and fear wins the battle.

When I look back on all the worries
I remember the story of the old man
who said on his deathbed
that he had a lot of trouble in his life,
most of which never happened.
—*Sir Winston Churchill*

It's when we are sinking that we find ourselves in need of God and it drives us to Him. Even in a raging storm the LORD is present to help us. None but the Creator of the waves could tread upon the waters of the sea. Just as the disciples yielded to the evidence, and confessed their faith, so must we in order to be saved.

We are born of God, taught of God, and anointed of God. He is our protective Father, our King, Who can call on thousands of angels to save us. We all need God's Spirit to fight our battles because we're not strong enough on our own. The indwelling of the Holy Spirit gives us the greatest defense against evil spirits that try to erode our faith and steal our serenity.

> *You are from God, little children,*
> *and have overcome them;*
> *because greater is He Who is in you*
> *than he who is in the world.*
> —1 John 4:4

Christ is the great Savior and we must come to Him for our salvation. Jesus has compassion for us no matter how scared or desperate we may feel. He will not only reassure that we have nothing to fear, but will extend His hand and help us cross over all fears in our path, no matter how great or small they may be. There's never a reason to despair or be afraid because we're assured of being victorious through all things when Christ is LORD of our lives.

> *I sought the LORD and He answered me,*
> *and rescued me from all my fears.*
> —Psalm 34:4

It can be helpful to remind ourselves that abiding in God's love and His salvation allows us a Light Who drives out darkness and fear. In addition to being our light and salvation, the LORD is the Defender of our lives. There's supernatural protection when the arms of Eternity are on our side.

> *The LORD is my light and my salvation;*
> *Whom should I fear?*
> *The LORD is the defense of my life;*
> *Whom should I dread?*
> —Psalm 27:1

Our Safe House

His loyal love supports;
His soothing touch makes us happy.

When I thought, My foot slips,
your steadfast love, O LORD, held me up.
—Psalm 94:18

Many of us, like King David, have had bouts of anxiety and know all too well its debilitating presence when it devours our peace and joy. What can we do when anxiety comes upon us?

In thee, O LORD, do I put my trust:
let me never be put to confusion.
Deliver me in thy righteousness,
and cause me to escape:
incline thine ear unto me, and save me.
Be thou my strong habitation,
whereunto I may continually resort:
thou hast given commandment to save me;
for thou art my rock and my fortress.
—Psalm 71:1-3

God is our rock and our safe house in Whom we can run to and feel secure no matter the danger. David felt liberty to plead to God—his Protector, Defender, and Friend—and we, too, may have the same confidence as believers. We are God's children and His promises are catered to us on a personal basis.

> *Incline Your ear to me, rescue me quickly;*
> *be a rock of strength for me,*
> *a stronghold to save me.*
> *—Psalm 31:2*

> *But You, LORD, are a shield around me,*
> *My glory, and the One Who lifts my head.*
> *—Psalm 3:3*

In the Scripture above we find David had a constant and steady helper—the LORD—when troubles weighed heavily. As a shield covers and defends the body from an enemy, so will God cover and defend when others rise up against us. During times of trouble when our heads are bowed down, as if overpowered by a weight, God promises to lift us up, relieving all of our distresses and helping us through our troubles.

The more we allow God's Word to fill our minds with lovely, pure, and hopeful thoughts, the more comfort we find when trying to take captive discouraging, sad, and negative thoughts. Psalm 94:19 reads: *When my anxious thoughts multiply within me, Your comfort delights my soul.* The Psalmist is aware that hopeful and despairing thoughts weave in and out of his mind, but he finds comfort and centering when he meditates on those thoughts pertaining to God—His wondrous grace, mercy, and His Divine light—his higher life, heavenward bound!

> *Cast your burden on the LORD,*
> *and He will sustain you.*
> *He will never permit*
> *the righteous to be moved.*
> *—Psalm 55:22*

When we lay all that troubles us on God's shoulders, He promises to carry us and bear our burdens. As long as we remain righteous, trusting, and dependent upon God, we will never be shaken—safe as if we're already with God in Heaven. This is an amazing promise of comfort for our ever-shifting and entangled minds.

Proverbs 12:25 reads: *Anxiety in a person's heart weighs it down, but a good word makes it glad.* This Scripture holds the key to helping a melancholy spirit that's breaking under a debilitating load of worry, fear, or sorrow. Let's be diligent in extending words of kindness and hope to those suffering under the heavy weight of anxious thoughts. Striving to enrich our minds with daily supplies of God's extravagant love, His immeasurable grace, His bountiful hope, His highest wisdom, and Holy inspiration is central to safeguarding our thoughts and ultimately protecting our soul.

> *Do not be anxious about anything,*
> *but in everything by prayer*
> *and pleading with thanksgiving*
> *let your requests be made known to God.*
> *And the peace of God,*
> *which surpasses all comprehension,*
> *will guard your hearts and minds in Christ Jesus.*
> *—Philippians 4:6-7*

God doesn't want us to be anxious about the cares of this world, but instead to have a devoted deposition of prayer with thanksgiving—at all times and in all circumstances. We can all recount God's Providential friendship in which He has bailed us out of other troubles, sparing us pain, loss, and humiliation. We can also be thankful when we were spared danger, death, and given unconditional love when we were undeserving.

Since God can see both physical and eternal, past, present and future, we'll be protected from dangers that we never knew were posing a threat. God already knows everything about us. He wants a relationship with us and that's why we should still talk to Him about all facets of our lives—the beautiful and the ugly, the good and the bad. We are privileged in being able to cry out to God—calling on His name—and being assured we'll be heard and delivered.

> *Rejoice in hope, be patient in tribulation,*
> *be constant in prayer.*
> *—Romans 12:12*

*The righteous cry out, and the LORD hears
and rescues them from all their troubles.*
—Psalm 34:17

Imagine how truly dreadful our anxieties would be if there were no God to whom we may go when we're in dire need and troubles abound. God does not promise to deliver us from all trouble on earth, even though He is most capable of doing so. The promise assures that every righteous person has complete deliverance from all trouble in the hereafter.

*These things I have spoken to you
so that in Me you may have peace.
In the world you have tribulation,
but take courage; I have overcome the world.*
—John 16:33

*Casting all your anxieties on Him,
because He cares for you.*
—1 Peter 5:7

Letting God have our anxieties and cares allows us a Savior Who involves Himself with all that concerns us as believers. Whether it be spiritual or temporal, great or small, God is there to help. What affects us, affects Him. We need not be anxious when we know God and how deeply He cherishes each of us. He promises He will sustain us.

Come close to God and He will come close to you.
—James 4:8

James 4:8 is reassurance that if our soul seeks God, He will meet with us there. We can approach God through prayer, and in reading His Word. We are certain to find mercy, love, blessings, and deliverance when we draw close to Him.

It may be helpful to remind ourselves that this world, and all its trouble, will be like a blink of an eye in comparison to our future home in Heaven. When tragedy strikes and I can't find serenity, nor a way to calm myself, I like to think of God stretching out a blanket and whispering, '*Run to me and I'll wrap you close to my heart until the storm passes. I'll never let you go, you're with Me forever.*'

> Now may the LORD of peace Himself give you peace at all times in every way. The LORD be with you all.
> —2 Thessalonians 3:16

Tender Regard

The sunshine of the LORD
Illumines our spirits
In eternal rays of hope.

We find in Psalm 41 that David was on his sick bed grieving over barbaric treatment from his enemies and the betrayal of friends. David found comfort, however, through God's promises of mercy and compassion. Psalm 41:1 reads: *Blessed is one who considers the helpless; The LORD will save him on a day of trouble.* His faith assured him of the LORD'S benevolent hand to lead him out of his troubles. Just as David was comforted and lifted up, so are we when our enemies try to harm us. God extends mercy, through others, with a hand to hold when we find ourselves desperate and distraught.

The word, *considers*, from the Scripture above implies endeavoring to seek out the helpless, looking into their circumstances, and being in the habit of doing so. And as such, we are to use our power and means to do good to those we find.

The Bible is full of God's mercy toward His created. The Hebrew word, *Hesed*, comes from a root word that means to bow one's head in courtesy to an equal. It is the idea of showing kindness above and beyond what is expected. *Hesed* conveys benevolence, patience and grace with fervent desire for someone. It also extends joy and zeal with loving favor.

Hesed is found nearly 250 times in the Bible. In all those instances, there is included the idea of the steadfastness and continuing nature of a long-lasting and abiding kindness. Since God has shown this deep ardent mercy toward us, we must extend it to others if we are to be like our Creator.

Each time we extend kindness, gentleness, and patience, whether it be a small gesture or big one, we are leaving pieces of God's heart with others. Each day of our lives should be spent seeking ways we can leave touches of kindness everywhere we go and with everyone we come in contact. Doing this not only encourages the receiver, but also the giver!

If you're struggling and feeling alone, remember there's help to be found. We must discard feelings of not deserving help or believing we've messed up beyond repair, and being too ashamed to reveal our personal truths. No matter the circumstances, the LORD will consider your case, and will send physical, emotional or spiritual supplies—whatever the need, it will be met. God prepares His followers to search for those who need Him and when they cross paths, they step in eagerly to extend mercy and means.

Perhaps there's a sin that seems impossible to overcome or has caused severe repercussions in your life, trust God today and He'll give you a hand to lead you out. If one has ever seen a woman crying while wearing mascara, they know how pitiful, sad, and dramatic it is. Many of us steer away from others seeing our ugly cry, as some have termed it. Sorrow and sin were never meant to be bottled. We must show the LORD our ugly cry; allow our wounds, grievous regrets, and our sinful selves to purge from within.

> *Is Ephraim My dear son?*
> *Is he a delightful child?*
> *Indeed, as often as I have spoken against him,*
> *I certainly still remember him;*
> *therefore My heart yearns for him;*
> *I will certainly have mercy on him,*
> *declares the LORD.*
> —Jeremiah 31:20

The Scripture above is one of the most tenderly affectionate attributions of God's heart toward His children. Ephraim, the ten tribes, sinned against God and rebelled against chastisement even as far back as their youth. But God went to great effort and pain, unwilling to give him up. He felt a *yearning* desire towards him; *hamu meai lo,* 'my bowels are agitated for him.' In other words, God had a deep tenderness stirring within Him and could only feel pity and love. He declared He would be affectionately merciful to Ephraim and not give up on them: *rachem arachamennu,* 'I will be *affectionately merciful to him, with tender mercy, saith the LORD.'*

Through God's patience, love, chastisement, and persistent encouragement, Ephraim eventually lamented their sins. God, their Father, loved them as His delighted child! Their hearts were impressionable and ready for God's instruction after seeing how desperately wicked their hearts were. God's grace and patience were not in vain.

Penitence is precious in God's sight and He will turn no remorseful soul away, no matter how unsightly they have become from the ravages of sin. John 6:37 reads: *Everything that the Father gives Me will come to Me, and the one who comes to Me I certainly will not cast out.* Even the angels rejoice over one sinner who repents (Luke 5:10).

God pursues His beloved children with a relentless passion. He will be their loyal Shepherd and Friend forever; nothing, not even death, will tear them away from God's deep abiding heart. Even if we have betrayed God countless times, He will always welcome us back! Our God abounds in beauty, grace, kindness, mercy, forgiveness, faithfulness, and loyal love!

> *Surely goodness and mercy shall follow me*
> *all the days of my life: and I will dwell*
> *in the house of the Lord for ever.*
> —Psalm 23:6

The Bible tells of a man who was struck with a withered hand. In Mark 3:5 Jesus said to the man, '*Stretch out your hand.*' He stretched it out, and his hand was restored. The man had to be willing to show the LORD his scars and have faith that Jesus would heal him. And so it is with us, we must allow the LORD to view the deepest and most vulnerable reaches of our heart. This can be a scary thing to do, and will require courage and raw honesty about who we are. Turning the contents of ourselves over to God in confession is powerful and deeply rewarding. This is why Satan tries to keep us hidden in the dark and trapped; he doesn't want us to experience God's transforming light or His compassionate love.

> *Though the black midnight overshadows my way,*
> *I will hold to the harbor of your love*
> *Where ten thousand candles burn along the shore.*

    Decide today that you'll no longer be held captive by the enemy. God urges us to confess and repent, embracing His light, allowing a painful, cathartic process to take place within our soul. Then fears, self-doubt, and feelings of self-loathing and hatred will be released.

    God's mercy and His renewing grace will heal the devastating destruction of sin. Whether we're the ones helping or suffering, God is faithful to bless and reward with His rich mercy and power.

> *With God's hope, we can lay down our souls*
> *And rest in the peaceful arms of God.*

Solace in Sorrow

There was no greater gift
Jesus could have given his friends
Than to die for their sins and then
Leave them with the breath of God.

He took Peter, James and John along with Him,
and He began to be deeply distressed and troubled.
'My soul is overwhelmed with sorrow
to the point of death,' He said
'Stay here and keep watch.'
—Mark 14:33-34

Jesus also experienced sorrow. In the garden of Gethsemane, on the night before His crucifixion, Jesus prayed with crushing sorrow for God to spare Him the horrifying death on the cross. Our Savior suffered fear, abandonment, and desperation. And while God heard His tearful pleadings, Jesus was not spared dying.

> So also you have sorrow now,
> but I will see you again,
> and your hearts will rejoice,
> and no one will take your joy from you.
> —John 16:22

The Scripture above portrays the account of Jesus reassuring His disciples He would see them again after His resurrection. We read in Luke that the apostles were sleeping for sorrow and seemingly unconcerned about their Master's grief. The disciples wept because they loved Jesus, and loved Him so much that they left everything to be His followers. They were likely exhausted, and heavy in heart, knowing their spiritual confidant and faithful friend was no longer going to be there in the flesh to soothe and encourage them.

> When He rose from prayer, He came to the disciples
> and found them sleeping from sorrow.
> —Luke 22:45

> Let not your heart be troubled;
> ye believe in God, believe also in me.
> —1 John 14:1

Jesus sought to console the disciples by reminding them that truth will allay all fear and give ultimate comfort to the soul. It's remarkable that Jesus knew their hearts and the perfect words to say to them. God will comfort us just as He comforted the apostles.

Jesus told the disciples earlier that He was going to die and rise again. He reassured them they would have the Holy Spirit after His resurrection. Jesus' words comforted and gave them hope.

> *I will not leave you as orphans; I am coming to you.*
> —John 14:18

What's incredible about Christ's ascension is that the apostles never doubted his resurrection from the dead. No persecution or trial ever shook their faith in their Savior, their beloved Friend. Each still had joy and it stayed behind within their spirit, despite their sorrow at knowing they were parting from Jesus in the earthly form.

> *I will never leave thee, nor forsake thee.*
> —Hebrews 13:5

The apostle reminds the believer that God will never leave them or forsake them. These same words were also spoken to Joshua. Joshua 1:5 reads: 'As I was with Moses, so will I be with thee; I will not fail thee, nor forsake thee.' They were also spoken by David to Solomon. 1 Chronicles 28:20 reads: And David said to Solomon his son, 'Be strong and of good courage, and do it: fear not, nor be dismayed: for the LORD God, even my God, will be with thee; He will not fail thee, nor forsake thee, until thou hast finished all the work for the service of the house of the LORD.' Just as these promises applied to the faithful of those who have gone on before us, they apply to us today.

As true believers, we have the gracious presence of God with us when we face temptation or adversity of any kind. God's reassuring words also remain with us at the time of our death and carry with us into Eternity. We can be assured of God helping us at all times and through anything!

> *Every blade in the field*
> *Every leaf in the forest*
> *Lays down its life in its season*
> *As beautifully as it was taken up.*
> —Henry David Thoreau

There are accounts of mourners who have died from *Takotsubo cardiomyopathy*, the medical term for Broken Heart Syndrome. Japanese physicians originated the diagnosis in 1990. The heart takes on the shape of a *takotsubo*, a Japanese fishing pot, or octopus pot. The syndrome can mimic the symptoms of a heart attack; the normal heart appears as if it has literally been broken.

When one experiences *Broken Heart Syndrome*, the body releases stress hormones that temporarily curb the heart's ability to pump as it should. Then a part of the heart, called the left ventricle, weakens, stretching out to form a narrow, neck-shaped section of the heart. Experts also believe that the coronary arteries, which feed oxygen to the heart muscle, spasm. As a result, chest pains can ensue with a momentary *freezing* or *stunning* of the heart, that in turn causes circulation issues.

If not treated, Broken Heart Syndrome can be as deadly as a heart attack. When death cannot be attributed to any other disease or malady, a medical determination will sometimes rule Broken Heart Syndrome as the cause of death for grief-stricken individuals.

Grief never gives us its schedule.

Grief often comes in waves and can leave us feeling as though we're suffocating. Though there is nothing anyone can say or do to rid the heart of the crushing weight of grief, homeopathic medicine, Ignatia Amara, can help to soften bereavement for some patients, and do so without harmful side effects. After taking Ignatia Amara 200C for a few weeks, mourners found that they were better able to work through the shock and aftermath of a devastating loss.

Perhaps you've lost the dearest person on earth and grief has left your days, and even your sleep, consumed of torrential tears. Know that at all times, you're under God's merciful regard. We have an empathetic ambassador in the beauty of Jesus' deeply abiding spirit.

Sweet By and By

For many years, the hymn, *Sweet By and By* has been a personal favorite. I love to sing the song in times of joy and in times of sorrow. The lyrics and melody touch me; as my teary eyes gaze upward, I anticipate a grand reunion with my eternal Father, and with all those I have missed terribly.

We learn from the history of this masterpiece that it was a collaboration between two friends, Sanford Fillmore Bennett and Joseph P. Webster. Sanford Bennett was a physician and lyricist at the time of the writing of this song. He observed that his friend, Joseph Webster, was a sensitive soul and plagued with bouts of depression. After taking notice of Joseph's shifting moods, Sanford wanted to help him.

Sanford enlisted the help of Joseph to write the music for his lyrical piece, *Sweet By and By*. He felt that giving Joseph something to work on would help to soothe his troubled soul, and it did! As soon as Sanford handed the complete hymn to Joseph, his spirit was lifted and he started writing the notes while playing his violin. This is a touching story of the light of hope triumphing over darkness and a sweet collaboration between two friends who needed each other!

Sweet By and By

There's a land that is fairer than day,
And by faith we can see it afar;
For the Father waits over the way
To prepare us a dwelling place there.

In the sweet by and by,
We shall meet on that beautiful shore;
In the sweet by and by,
We shall meet on that beautiful shore.

We shall sing on that beautiful shore
The melodious songs of the blest;
And our spirits shall sorrow no more,
Not a sigh for the blessing of rest.

To our bountiful Father above,
We will offer our tribute of praise
For the glorious gift of His love
And the blessings that hallow our days.

—Sanford Fillmore Bennett

Tears Took Your Soul

Your pain swirled an ocean;
Its tears took your soul
It never crossed my mind,
You'd ever let go.

I would've been your solace,
Your place to hide
From the fears
Tearing through your mind.

No matter how hard I try, can't dry
Tears welling in my eyes
Your memory's all I've left to treasure
Of our time spent together.

Your silence shears me deeply;
It haunts in waves of sorrow
Then comes and hurts me—all over—
Again tomorrow.

I pray your soul is sailing,
Sailing on the sea,
Forever sailing
In the arms of sweet serenity.

Angelic Comfort

*Then I looked, and I heard the voices of many angels
around the throne
and the living creatures and the elders;
and the number of them was myriads of myriads,
and thousands of thousands,
saying with a loud voice,
'Worthy is the Lamb Who was slaughtered
to receive power, wealth, wisdom, might, honor,
glory, and blessing.'
—Revelation 5:11-12*

Mary Magdalene found Jesus' tomb empty after His death. As she stood weeping, she saw two angels. John 20:12 reads: *And she saw two angels in white, sitting where the body of Jesus had lain, one at the head and one at the feet.* God offers His pure and selfless love through the use of His angels. These heavenly beings surround and worship Him near His throne—thousands upon thousands are close to Him and come from Him. They enlighten and protect the believer in all their ways.

We find in John 20 that Mary also saw Jesus standing outside the tomb. He said to her, *'Touch me* not; for I am not yet ascended to my Father: but go to my brethren, and say unto them, I ascend unto my Father, and your Father; and to my God, and your God.' Mary told the disciples she had seen the LORD. Then at evening, on the first day of the week, when the doors were shut where the disciples were assembled for fear of the Jews, Jesus stood in their midst, and said to them, 'Peace be unto you.' He showed them His hands and His side. The disciples rejoiced when they saw the LORD. *Jesus breathed on them and said to them, 'Receive the Holy Spirit'* (John 20:22).

> *The chariots of God are twenty thousand,*
> *even thousands of angels:*
> *the LORD is among them, as in Sinai,*
> *in the Holy place.*
> —Psalm 68:17

The word angel appears 285 times in the King James Bible, beginning in the book of Genesis to the concluding book of Revelation. Angels attend to dying saints and carry them to glory. Luke 16:22 reads: *Now it happened that the poor man (Lazarus) died and was carried away by the angels to Abraham's arms (bosom).* Some on their deathbeds have spoken or gestured to indicate unseen beings were arriving. Even animals seem to have a heightened sense of the afterlife, according to some.

When my son's guinea pig was moments away from death, he stood on his back paws and reached up as if to touch something above his head with his front paws. Did Sparky see a glimpse of the unknown, an angel perhaps, and was reaching to touch him? None of us can say for certain that angels are around the dying because we can't see them. But if the account of Lazarus in Abraham's bosom is an indication, we have nothing to fear when our earthly life is closing. These merciful, unseen, angelic hands gently take the pure of heart back to God so that His Divine Providence is fulfilled.

   I can recall being in a children's home and finding later that the home was supported by people who gave funds to supply our needs while living in Sunshine Lodge. Even though I never saw the people or what monetary means they had supplied, that does not mean I wasn't helped by unknown benefactors. God created angels to minister, encourage, and impart wisdom.

   1 Kings 19 tells the story of Elijah running from evil Jezebel and wishing to die. As he lay asleep under a broom tree, an angel touched him and said, *'Arise, eat!'* He awoke and saw a round loaf of bread baked on hot coals, and a pitcher of water. So he ate and drank, and lay down again. The angel of the LORD returned and touched him again, saying, *'Arise, eat; because the journey is too long for you.'* So he ate and drank, and journeyed in the strength of that food for forty days and forty nights to Horeb, the mountain of God. We see from this touching story that God cherishes and takes great care of us. He will use whatever means He chooses to ensure His plans and purposes are accomplished. We can

search the world over, but we'll never find a truer, purer, more compassionate friend than that of God!

> *For the Son of Man is going to come in the glory of*
> *His Father with His angels,*
> *and will then repay every person*
> *according to his deeds.*
> *—Matthew 16:27*

Many believe the LORD'S return is near. God has not revealed the hour of Christ's return, not even the angels know, and they are privy to the eternal world as they circle around the throne of God. Our lives are fragile and we're not promised our next breath, but if we choose to live for our Creator, we'll go with Him to live forever when He returns with His angels.

> *But of that day and that hour knoweth no man,*
> *no, not the angels who are in Heaven,*
> *neither the Son, but the Father.*
> *—Mark 13:32*

If you have not lived as you should, why not repent and turn your life over to Christ? Don't worry that you don't have it all together and won't be accepted. The LORD is a Physician to all and does not prefer one over another (Luke 5:31). Providence is on your side. Don't be afraid of the shame you hide, show it to God and trust someone with the contents of your heart so that you can find your way home.

There's great comfort to be found in Hebrews 1:14, it reads: *Are they not all ministering spirits, sent forth to minister for them who shall be heirs of salvation?* Did you catch that, *heirs of salvation?* Accepting Jesus as the LORD of your life, repenting of your sins, and coming out of the grave of sin, through the burial of baptism to a new resurrected life, allows you to become God's heir.

God delights to welcome you home where He waits to lavish you with serenity and all of the treasures Heaven contains! Don't put off making your heart right with God and risk losing it all. Nothing in this world is worth more than your soul. Great peace is yours when you take up your cross and follow the LORD; you'll be prepared, with nothing to fear, when the LORD returns with His angels to take the faithful. Let's all get ready now to embrace our beautiful LORD.

Imagine what it would be like if someone you once loved, and is now dead, came back to see you? Many of us have loved-ones we grieve and miss every day. *Just one more time,* we often say, *to see, touch, and embrace them.* Even though in our physical world we'll never have that opportunity, we can take to heart that on the other side of Eternity, we'll also rise and meet our saved loved ones. And it won't be a momentary encounter, no, it will be forever! And what's even more beautiful about the anticipated reunion, is we'll meet God, face to face, surrounded in His magnificent radiance. Jesus will embrace us and we'll be loved, and kept safe in a world without end. I want a world like that and I know you do too!

Neither can they die any more:
for they are equal unto the angels;
and are the children of God
being the children of the resurrection.
—Luke 20:34-36

Seal Upon His Heart

There's no burden too heavy for God,
There's no place too far
When He pursues His children.

When I awake, I am still with Thee
and in Thy likeness.
—Psalm 17, 139

For those of us whose mothers have passed away, we know they never leave our hearts and are never far from our thoughts. At any time, we can bring forth their memory and find great comfort in reminiscing about time spent with them.

Whenever I look at my son's hands, I think of my mother. Her alabaster hands were perfectly shaped and graceful, much like what we may think of as professional pianist having; he elegantly touches his audience with chords that evoke beauty and memory.

When my son was a child and I held his hand, I felt as though I were holding onto my mother's hand too. Through the years, my son's hands have been a blessing and a gentle reminder of my dear mother's presence. Even now in death, mom comforts me whenever I remember her milky-white, artfully shaped, comforting hands. I feel blessed that God designed my son's hands in my mother likeness; they are both endeared treasures. Those memories spent holding their supple hands bring a smile as I fondly think of them.

Scripture speaks a lot about God's hands and the power behind His indescribable love and care. Deeper than an earthly mother is God's devotion to His children. Psalm 73:23 is a powerful Scripture regarding God's loving hands, it reads: *Nevertheless I am continually with You; You have taken hold of my right hand.* It's a great comfort knowing that *it is God* Who takes hold of our hand and never lets go! He remains as our ultimate Protector and Friend throughout our earthly lives and forever in Eternity.

> *Many, LORD my God, are the wonders*
> *which You have done,*
> *and Your thoughts toward us; there is no one to*
> *compare with You.*
> *If I would declare and speak of them, they would be*
> *too numerous to count.*
> —Psalm 40:5

I have come to view my tragic past differently today after reflecting upon God's hands and knowing how He has carried me through the years. I recall the loss of my former home and those early weeks when I was taken to live in a children's home, and later, foster homes.

I cried desperately for my mother and father's touch again; to have my family, despite how broken it was. In those wee hours, I didn't know God was with me. All I could really see then was the searing pain and the isolation from the dearest on earth to me. And even though a broken home was not God's plan for my life, He was still there in the shattered places.

Now as I revisit those frightening nights when I was first taken from my parents, I believe the LORD was cradling my heart as I lay fearful, confused, and profoundly forsaken. In it all, His hand had never left me.

> LORD, You have searched me and known me.
> You know when I sit down and when I get up;
> You understand my thought from far away.
> You scrutinize my path and my lying down,
> And are acquainted with all my ways.
> Even before there is a word on my tongue,
> Behold, LORD, You know it all.
> You have encircled me behind and in front,
> And placed Your hand upon me.
> Such knowledge is too wonderful for me;
> It is too high, I cannot comprehend it.
> —Psalm 139:1-6

There's comfort in knowing God takes deep interest in us, so much so, that we are engraved on His palm and constantly with Him. The faithful are all seals upon God's heart and are His dear, cherished children. Because of His sacred love for me, I'm looking forward to the day I meet our loving Father face to face. I long for the moment He cups my face with His tender hands, and tells me He has always loved me and I'm home. I know you, too, anticipate this glorious, upcoming event! But until that grand day, let's not forget how deeply devoted God's heart is toward us and how safe we truly are because we're always on His mind and ever in His sight!

> *Behold, I have inscribed you*
> *on the palms of My hands;*
> *Your walls are continually before Me.*
> *—Isaiah 49:16*

Tender Mercies

At dawn or in the ebony of night,
God is a stillness permeating our souls
Despite any storm waging without.

Deep calls to deep at the sound of Your waterfalls;
all Your breakers and Your waves
have passed over me.
The LORD will send His goodness in the daytime;
and His song will be with me in the night,
a prayer to the God of my life.
—Psalm 42:7-8

David expected his deliverance to come from God's favor. Although his situation was bad—one affliction coming upon another, one frightful thought summoning another, and a mountain of grief overwhelming him—he knew there would be a calm after the storm. This assurance supported and encouraged David as he remembered that God would command His lovingkindness.

At times it can appear that God has hidden His face from us, but we are never out of His view. Job 36:7 is testament to that promise, it reads: *He does* not take His eyes off the righteous. Jeremiah 31:3 affirms that *we are loved with an everlasting love*, a love that never fails and nothing separates. With loving kindness, God draws us into His covenant, His solemn oath, where we have communion with Him—His Spirit upon our souls. We are sanctified and set apart as sons and daughters of the most high. What amazing and indescribable affection God has for us! He longs to reveal the secrets of His heart.

> *The secret of the Lord is for those who fear Him,*
> *And He will make them know His covenant.*
> *—Psalm 25:14*

> *Withhold not thou thy tender mercies*
> *from me, O LORD:*
> *let thy loving-kindness and thy truth*
> *continually preserve me.*
> *—Psalm 40:11*

Tender mercies implies propensities and feelings as a mother extends toward her child. We learn from this beautiful verse that God is our complete family, both Father and Mother.

> *My friends are my scoffers;*
> *my eye weeps to God.*
> *—Job 16:20*

We find in the verse above that Job's friends misunderstood and scorned him during his trials. His friends set themselves as his spiritual counselors and they misinterpreted the workings of

God and Job's integrity. No one but God can truly understand the heart and mind of another. Instead of casting blame or speculating on the reasons for Job's adversity, his three friends should have reminded him of his goodness and recounted examples of how his life had honored God and His people. We should be careful and tread gently when advising and counseling others because we cannot be as wise as God and comprehend His unsearchable ways. God's tracks cannot be traced nor His dealings fully revealed. He is the Infinite Spirit without limits, with no beginning or end. We should not sit in judgment of God's doings or presume we know what He's thinking and what is best.

> *You walked through the sea;*
> *You passed through the surging waters,*
> *but left no footprints.*
> *—Psalm 77:19*

> *The secret things belong to the Lord our God,*
> *but the things that are revealed belong to us*
> *and to our children forever,*
> *that we may do all the words of this law.*
> *—Deuteronomy 29:29*

Despite Job's friends failing to assess his heart and his circumstances correctly, Job clearly knew Whom he could trust and find compassion—God, His Father. Job poured out his tears to God, the One Who knew and understood him fully. He surrendered his broken heart to God and was met with healing and ease of his troubled spirit.

Hannah also grieved greatly. 1 Samuel 1:10 reads: *She, greatly distressed, prayed to the LORD and wept bitterly.* She refused to eat because she had not been able to conceive a child. We also find that her husband, Elkanah, did not fully grasp her pain when suggesting he was better to her than ten sons. He was likely in pain too and loved his wife, and thought he was doing his best to console her.

Tears mingled with Hannah's prayer as she pleaded to the tender mercy of God. She vowed that if He would bless her with a child, she would dedicate him to the LORD all of his days. It's further recorded that Eli, the priest, saw her praying and thought she was drunk with wine because he couldn't hear her words; he only saw her lips quivering as she wept and prayed. After discovering she was not intoxicated, but instead distressed, Eli reassured her that God would grant her request. Hannah believed God would accept her pleading and give her His best. And the LORD remembered her and blessed her with a son. She named him Samuel, whose name means, *Heard by God.*

The Messiah also wept in agony. Luke 22:44 reads: *And being in agony He prayed more earnestly; and His sweat became like great drops of blood falling down to the ground.* There has been speculation as to what the Scripture meant by 'great drops of blood'. Some scholars believe the anguish was so intense that Jesus experienced Hematidrosis, a very rare medical condition that causes one to ooze or sweat blood from the skin when they're not cut or injured. Extreme anguish can cause the tiny blood vessels around the glands to constrict and then dilate to the point of rupture, thus causing blood to effuse into the sweat glands. It is possible that this is an accurate description due to the fact that Luke was a physician and penned the travail of our LORD. In contrast, others believe this could merely be a simile describing Jesus' sweat falling to the ground in heavy drops much like blood drips from a severe wound.

Matthew and Mark describe Jesus' suffering *'To the point of death'*. Whether it was actual blood drops or not, Jesus was fully aware of what was ahead for Him and knew his suffering was going to be horrific and brutal. Isaiah 52:14 reads, *Just as many were appalled at you, My people, so His appearance was marred beyond that of a man, and His form beyond the sons of mankind.* Jesus was unrecognizable when the tormentors and murderers were done with Him. Christ knew this years ahead and still chose to die, pure and sinless for all of mankind.

In the example of Christ's travail, we find an empathetic and timeless Mediator Who is able to make intercession on our behalf. Prayer is an outlet of ease for our souls and we can be sure we never seek the LORD just to find emptiness and confusion in return. We are blessed with peace, comfort, and strength even if our prayers are not answered as we had expected, or in the time we desired.

When our souls are nourished
Deeply in God's heart,
Our spirit blossoms and blooms
Then our petals fall completely
In love with our LORD.

We can encourage ourselves with God's reassuring promises when trials come. In keeping hope alive in our hearts, we won't be destroyed; for the waves and billows are under His Divine awareness. Our awesome God can command down the raging seas, and they will obey Him.

And grieve not the Holy Spirit of God,
whereby ye are sealed unto the day of redemption.
—Ephesians 4:30

The Holy Spirit is part of the trinity of God Almighty—Deity—and is a spirit of light, truth, and comfort. Christians are warned to not grieve the Holy Spirit. Grieve (λυπέω, llupeó) in the Scripture above means to distress or afflict with sorrow. Many of us grieve the Holy Spirit when we sin, berate and make fun of others, have an argumentative or cynical disposition, tell unsavory jokes and stories, entertain licentious thoughts and desires, have an ungrateful heart, or discourage others in being true to their principles. We can also be the cause for others to become discouraged, depressed, and possibly lose their faith if we neglected to extend mercy, support, and benevolence or were insensitive to their pain and suffering.

One may ask, how can we know that we've grieved the Holy Spirit? Having knowledge and wisdom in the Word of God allows us to discern good and evil. We can also have an inner turmoil, even to the point of becoming ill, when we've violated the sensitive part of God's spirit. It's good to pray and ask God for discernment if we become uneasy or fearful about any actions or thoughts we may have experienced. If doubt, sadness, or foreboding accompany any part of our heart, it's time to evaluate the root cause of those feelings.

Grieving the Holy Spirit is a very serious matter because it can thwart God's plans and purposes for our lives. The Holy Spirit can be grieved when we disregard and abuse the precious gift of God dwelling within. We'd all be wise to evaluate our actions so as to not bring sorrow upon our souls or anyone else. A lack of compassion for the suffering of others has the potential to drive away the Holy Spirit in others. Father God grieves when we go our own way, sin against Him, or leave His protective presence. We are God's seals who belong to the LORD and designed for His Divine purposes.

> *Let thy tender mercies come unto me,*
> *that I may live: for thy law is my delight.*
> —Psalm 119:77

It's a great comfort to know that if others slight our grief, God never will. Even when others misunderstand our integrity or make light of our suffering, God is there to nurture while providing the truer glimpse of ourselves.

God is the mighty fortress of our life, there's no good thing that we can't expect from Him. Every day the LORD extends his loving-kindness—His overflowing and superabundant mercy! During the night we can sing of God's mercy and goodness while leaving our worries with Him when we close our eyelids in prayer.

> *Now behold, I have made you today*
> *like a fortified city*
> *and like a pillar of iron and walls of bronze*
> *against the whole land,*
> *to the kings of Judah, to its leaders, to its priests,*
> *and to the people of the land.*
> *And they will fight against you,*
> *but they will not overcome you,*
> *for I am with you to save you, declares the LORD.*
> —Jeremiah 1:18-19

The Sands of Time are Sinking

The sands of time are sinking;
The dawn of heaven breaks;
The summer morn I've sighed for,
The fair sweet morn awakes;
Dark, dark has been the midnight,
But dayspring is at hand,
And glory, glory dwelleth
In Emmanuel's land.

The King there in His beauty
Without a veil is seen;
It were a well-spent journey,
Though trials lay between:
The Lamb with His fair army
On Zion's mountain stands,
And glory, glory dwelleth
In Emmanuel's land.

O Christ, He is the fountain,
The deep, sweet well of love!
The streams on earth I've tasted;
More deep I'll drink above:
There to an ocean fullness
His mercy doth expand,
And glory, glory dwelleth
In Emmanuel's land.

The bride eyes not her garment,
But her dear bridegroom's face;
I will not gaze at glory,
But on my King of grace;
Not at the crown He giveth,
But on His pierced hands;
The Lamb is all the glory
Of Emmanuel's land.

—Samuel Rutherford, Anne Ross

Face of Light

*Our Morning Star is a beautiful treasure box
Of extravagant and timeless jewels.*

*The people who walked in darkness
have seen a great light;
those who dwelt in a land of deep darkness,
on them has light shone.
—Isaiah 9:2*

There are only two rulers of this world, God and Satan. God is an all encompassing light in Whom no one can see His face and live. He exudes joy, hope, mercy, peace, and unfailing love, yet Satan is darker than night, he's actually pitch blackness. Pitch black, as defined in the dictionary, is described as *extremely dark or black, being without moon light, and gloomy*. Satan is hopeless, evil, and the father of all lies. Fortunately we can be saved from the dismal gloom of Satan by choosing to walk as children of Holy God—our Father of Light.

There is no shifting shadow in Your Light.

The prophesies of old are like a candle in a dark room or on an obscure road at night that enable us to see things that otherwise would be invisible. We can have assurance that in God's prophetic light we are safely guided through dangerous, dark, and unknown places. All shadows are dispelled and every land of deep darkness is destroyed, forever. I want to be a part of that beautiful city of light and I know you do too!

> *We have also a more sure word of prophecy;*
> *whereunto ye do well that ye take heed,*
> *as unto a light that shineth in a dark place,*
> *until the day dawn, and the Day Star*
> *arise in your hearts.*
> —2 Peter 1:19

> *Because of the tender mercy of our God,*
> *with which the Sunrise from on high*
> *will visit us, to shine on those who*
> *sit in darkness and the shadow of death,*
> *to guide our feet into the way of peace.*
> —Luke 1:77-79

The Messiah is the morning Light, the rising Sun, (*anatolē*). He is our Dawn—Whose lit path leads our soul out of darkness and into restoration. Through Christ, the tender mercy of God has gifted us with a clear, true light that guides our steps. We need only to look up to His radiance, and stay in His holiness to be rescued and healed. It's a beautiful thought to know we're embraced with light from on high!

> *And the city has no need of the sun*
> *or of the moon to shine on it,*
> *for the glory of God has illuminated it,*
> *and its lamp is the Lamb.*
> —Revelation 21:23

Jesus, our sacrificial Lamb of Light—the One Whose face we are to behold—will one day return and receive us to Himself. On that glorious day, our Savior, our Day Star, will rise in splendor and take us to Heaven with Him. There death and darkness will have all been swallowed up in the victorious all-encompassing light of God. Then all of God's prophecies will have been fulfilled as we're transported to the beautiful harbor of our everlasting home!

> *LORD God of armies, restore us;*
> *make Your face shine upon us*
> *and we will be saved.*
> —Psalm 80:19

The Psalm above also applies to us today. We, too, can ask God to redeem us from our captivities, whether they be emotional, physical, or spiritual. We can take great comfort and reassurance that God can call on His innumerable hosts from both worlds—heavenly or earthly—to save and bless us. As we pray for Him to reconcile and snatch us out of the darkness of this world, His radiant face will smile upon us. And in His Light, all traces of hopelessness, despair, and condemnation will be removed, for it cannot exist in His presence.

And I will bring the blind by a way
that they knew not;
I will lead them in paths that they have not known:
I will make darkness light before them,
and crooked things straight.
These things will I do unto them,
and not forsake them.
—Isaiah 42:16

It is a known fact that light can have healing properties. Just think about the sun, when it's in view we feel better with inspiration. Some of us even experience a lessening of aches and pains in our bodies. Let's resolve to step into the light of God and share it with others, so that we are bathed in the resplendent glory of His eternal being.

The LORD bless you, and keep you;
the LORD cause His face to shine on you,
and be gracious to you;
the LORD lift up His face to you,
and give you peace.
—Numbers 6:24-26

Brightly beams our Father's mercy
From his lighthouse evermore,
But to us He gives the keeping
Of the lights along the shore.
—Philip Paul Bliss

Holy, Holy, Holy!

Holy, holy, holy! LORD God Almighty!
Early in the morning our song shall rise to Thee;
Holy, holy, holy! merciful and mighty!
God in three Persons, blessed Trinity!

Holy, holy, holy! all the saints adore Thee,
Casting down their golden crowns around the glassy sea;
Cherubim and seraphim, falling down before Thee,
Which wert and art and evermore shalt be.

Holy, holy, holy! though the darkness hide Thee,
Though the eye of sinful man Thy glory may not see;
Only Thou art holy, there is none beside Thee,
Perfect in pow'r, in love, and purity.

Holy, holy, holy! LORD God Almighty!
All Thy works shall praise Thy name, in earth and sky and sea;
Holy, holy, holy! merciful and mighty!
God in three Persons, blessed Trinity!

—Reginald Heber

Contrite Heart

> And immediately, while he was still speaking,
> a rooster crowed.
> And then the LORD turned and looked at Peter.
> And Peter remembered the word of the LORD,
> how He had told him,
> 'Before a rooster crows today,
> you will deny Me three times.'
> And he went out and wept bitterly.
> —Luke 22:60-62

The Scripture above portrays the account of Peter denying Jesus. Just after hearing the rooster crow, Peter realized what he had done. The LORD turned and looked upon him. Peter had disowned Christ, but Christ had not disowned him. Jesus was aware of the betrayal, but it was His eyes upon Peter that allowed him to know Jesus was still his friend.

To have denied Jesus three times was a horrible offense, but Christ would not call to him and shame or expose him, nor did he ridicule or make demands of him. He only gave Peter a look and in that moment when their eyes met, Peter likely wanted to throw his arms around Jesus' neck, sobbing while begging for forgiveness. He had to live with what he had done to the dearest friend he would ever have, and at a distance from the one Whose only opinion of him mattered. The exchange of glances between Jesus and Peter melted the apostle's heart into tears of Godly sorrow for his sin. Even though Christ was already arrested and on His way to His death, He remained gentle to all who had betrayed and hurt Him.

It was the grace of God that recovered Peter and brought him back to honoring his Savior. Peter was a devout follower, but this story allows all of us to take a deeper view into our own frailty and the things we boast before God. We can observe, too, that Jesus takes more notice of what we say and do than we may think. It's wonderful to know that Christ does not forsake us as we often forsake Him.

In this story of Peter's betrayal of the son of God, we see a frail man who admits his mistake and takes action to make it right. In the end, the apostle rose up stronger and exemplified tenderness through his contrite heart. Jesus called ordinary, frail men to be His disciples. He knew beforehand that Peter would ultimately turn his weakness into strength with boldness. To see a man weep at his own mistakes is a beautiful thing to behold in the eyes of the LORD.

Whisper of God

For in Him we live, and move, and have our being;
as certain also of your own poets have said,
for we are also His offspring.
—Acts 17:28

We are born of God and dependent upon His Providence. His patience, pity, and fatherly love sustains our fragile being; He upholds us through each moment. Without God, we can do nothing, and without of His saving grace, we are nothing. His goodness remains with the pure of heart and they have no worry of being abandoned or destroyed, ever!

So He said, 'Go out and stand on the mountain
before the LORD.'
And behold, the LORD was passing by!
And a great and powerful wind
was tearing out the mountains
and breaking the rocks in pieces before the LORD;
but the LORD was not in the wind.
And after the wind there was an earthquake,
but the LORD was not in the earthquake.
And after the earthquake, a fire,
but the LORD was not in the fire;

> *and after the fire, a sound of a gentle blowing.*
> *When Elijah heard it, he wrapped his face*
> *in his cloak and went out*
> *and stood in the entrance of the cave.*
> *And behold, a voice came to him and said,*
> *"What are you doing here, Elijah?"*
> —1 Kings 19:11-13

When we feel beaten down or discouraged in our spiritual pursuits, it can be helpful to remind ourselves of the life of Elijah. Elijah was a faithful prophet who knew the greatness of God. His vision allowed him to help restore God's reign in Israel. He fought hard and earnest accomplishing a great victory at Mt. Carmel. Despite this, he was still a man with frailty. He expected his victory to turn the king and the people away from the false god, Baal, but it did not.

Elijah's situation worsened when the queen, Jezebel, decided to murder him, attempting to get even for killing the prophets of Baal. Jezebel threatened and chased Elijah and he began to waiver in his faith. He questioned why God had become quiet, as if He was not concerned with what he was going through. He went to God with questions, but God didn't show up the way he had wanted him to, with great power and might. Nor did God reprimand Elijah with harsh words.

The LORD led the discouraged prophet to Mt. Sinai, a lonely mountain in the middle of the wilderness. This was also the same mountain in which Moses had met with God to receive the law of God. At Mt. Sinai God told Elijah to go out and stand on the mountain before the LORD. God knew Elijah needed a personal encounter with Him. He brought Himself to Elijah, but He was not in the wind, the earthquake or the fire. No, God was in the gentle silence. Did you catch that it wasn't the wind, earthquake, or the fire that caused Elijah to cover his face? It was the still voice of God instead!

Sometimes we can be like Elijah and only look for God in remarkable and powerful manifestations, and miss the Divine whisper Who wants to lead us. Even though God is capable of manifesting Himself in a powerful and dramatic way, it's often the gentle approach that opens hearts. Jesus Christ is the gentle Savior, and we can connect with Him through the Spirit of God. Then we, like Elijah, can expect God to reveal Himself in a gentle whisper.

> *Then he said to me, This is the word of the LORD to Zerubbabel, saying, 'Not by might nor by power, but by My Spirit,' says the LORD of armies.*
> *—Zachariah 4:6*

God was concerned with every detail of Elijah's life, from his smallest accomplishment to his greatest; He also extends the same care for each of us. The story of Elijah shows us a God Who is powerfully gentle and full of mercy.

Jesus gave Himself up meekly and gently to save all of us—that's amazing and transforming power! And just as He lulled the agitated sea for His disciples, extending a hand to hold them, He will also soothe the swirling current on the turbulent sea of our lives.

> *He made the storm be still,*
> *and the waves of the sea were hushed.*
> *Then they were glad that the waters were quiet,*
> *and he brought them to their desired haven.*
> —Psalm 107:29-30

Many of us have had, currently have, or will have an emotional, physical, or spiritual wilderness. Like Elijah, God may call us to meet with Him in the stillness of the wilderness too. We may then be urged to proceed in God's perspective, His time, and His plans while forsaking our own preconceived ideas. Embracing stillness allows room for God to meet and talk with us. It's then that we can be vessels, open and ready, to hear the beautiful whispers of God speaking through our spirit.

> *Blessed assurance, Jesus is mine!*
> *Oh, what a foretaste of glory divine!*
> *Heir of salvation, purchase of God,*
> *Born of His Spirit, washed in His blood.*
> —Fanny J. Crosby

Can We Start Over?

*Remember not the former things,
nor consider the things of old.
Behold, I am doing a new thing;
now it springs forth, do you not perceive it?
I will make a way in the wilderness
and rivers in the desert.*
—Isaiah 43:18-19

Out of the mouth of babes often comes powerful truths and insight. Years ago after my son was having a difficult morning, he said, 'Mom, *can we start over?*' I wrapped my arms around him and said, '*Of course!*' I've since pondered my son's words, 'Can we start over?' Does it not amaze you the innocence of children? They don't usually dwell on negativity for long, nor do they hold grudges. Most dole out forgiveness and generosity without thinking twice. I was impressed that my son didn't feel the need to string together a long drawn out explanation for his behavior. He simply wanted another chance. Those four words eradicated the troubles of that day and nothing was ever mentioned of it again.

It would be unrealistic to expect every problem to be solved by just expressing those four simple words, but it can be a first step. If we would endorse being like children when it comes to conflict, the world would be filled with happier relationships. Children can teach us that when a problem is brewing, we can simply make a request to start over.

> *Truly I say to you, unless you change*
> *and become like children,*
> *you will not enter the kingdom of Heaven.*
> *—Matthew 18:3*

To a great extent, children are free of pride, grudges, and haughtiness; they are characteristically humble and teachable. We learn from the Scripture above that Jesus admonished His disciples to be like them in those respects. We must seek to be humble and put others before ourselves.

> *Blessed are the meek:*
> *for they shall inherit the earth.*
> *—Matthew 5:5*

Meekness is not only a characteristic of children, but it's also one of the gifts of the spirit. Jesus spoke of meekness in the Bible when He said:

> *Take my yoke upon you, and learn of Me;*
> *for I am meek and lowly in heart:*
> *and ye shall find rest unto your souls.*
> *—Matthew 11:29*

Christ was the epitome of meekness. He had compassion on those whom others had cast out, or ridiculed. Jesus took hold of their hand and opened His heart of understanding toward them. The care He had toward His twelve disciples allowed us to see this. Jesus chose His followers from the seaside, not from a court or scholarly school. He was mild and gentle with them, and brought out their best. He didn't make an example of their mistakes either.

The word *meek* comes from the old Anglo-Saxon *meca*, or *meccea*, which means *a companion or equal*. A meek man has a gentle spirit and does not consider himself superior to others. You won't see him shove others aside or demand their way. He is a quiet, selfless, and yielding individual who has surrendered himself to God. He's well aware that what he has, he's received from the bounty of God, having never deserved any favor.

Meekness allows one to be patient when injury is brought upon him because he accepts and understands that vengeance belongs to God, and He will repay (Romans 12:19). A meek man does not engage sudden anger, malice, or long-harbored vengeance. He has pity for those who suffer even if they are his enemies. The meekness of a pure heart won't allow itself to become like a troubled sea that cannot flow serenely, whose waters billow.

Christ was lowly in heart. He humbled Himself so that He could teach poor scholars, and novices. No matter how seasoned we are in our walk with the LORD, we are still God's children and in need of our Father's constant oversight, wisdom, and eternal mercies. Where there is pride and anger, mental agony ensues, but a meek and lowly spirit finds all things smooth and peaceable. When we bow our heads with humility, regarding ourselves as empty vessels, we can then be filled with an abundance of wisdom and grace from Christ.

If we're paying attention
And ready to receive God's truths,
He'll print them on our heart and mind.

For the LORD taketh pleasure in His people:
He will beautify the meek with salvation.
—Psalm 149:4

Having a docile soul for God is both very lovely and deeply painful. We must get alone with God every day and allow Him, through His wisdom and Holy words, to guide our paths and change our hearts to become like Him. Seeking God's pure wisdom and His peace-loving ways will sustain us during the trials of our faith. As we learn more about God's heart, we can extend those attributes to others.

But the wisdom from above is first pure,
then peaceable, gentle, open to reason,
full of mercy and good fruits, impartial and sincere.
—James 3:17

Letters Before God

Isaiah 36-37 tells of Sennacherib, king of Assyria, a blasphemous and brutal king, who threatened and conquered nations. He sent a letter to Hezekiah—a God-fearing king who ruled Judah—indicating plans to destroy Jerusalem. Sennacherib downplayed Jehovah's power while extolling his own. He boasted of his victory over the Jewish king, Hezekiah, attempting to frighten him into surrender.

After Hezekiah heard the report of destruction planned against his people, he was distressed; tore his clothes, covered himself with sackcloth, and entered the house of the LORD. Then he sent Eliakim, who was in charge of the household, Shebna, the scribe, and the elders of the priests, covered with sackcloth, to Isaiah the prophet. And they said to him, *'This is what Hezekiah says: This day is a day of distress, rebuke, and humiliation; for children have come to the point of birth, and there is no strength to deliver them. Perhaps the LORD your God will hear the words of Rabshakeh, whom his master, the king of Assyria, has sent to taunt the living God, and will avenge the words which the*

LORD your God has heard. Therefore, offer a prayer for the remnant that is left.' Hezekiah went up to the house of the LORD, and spread the letter before the LORD. He prayed:

> 'O LORD of hosts, God of Israel,
> enthroned above the cherubim,
> You are the God, You alone,
> of all the kingdoms of the earth;
> You have made Heaven and earth.
> Incline Your ear, O LORD, and hear;
> open Your eyes, O LORD, and see;
> and hear all the words of Sennacherib,
> which he has sent to mock the living God.
> Truly, O LORD, the kings of Assyria
> have laid waste all the nations
> and their lands, and have cast their gods
> into the fire. For they were no gods,
> but the work of men's hands, wood and stone.
> Therefore they were destroyed.
> So now, O LORD our God, save us from his hand,
> that all the kingdoms of the earth may know that
> You alone are the LORD.'

The angel of the LORD went out and struck down 185,000 in the camp of the Assyrians. And when people arose early in the morning, behold, these were all dead bodies. Then Sennacherib departed and returned home and lived at Nineveh. And as he was worshiping in the house of Nisroch his god, his sons, Adrammelech and Sharezer, struck him down with the sword. And after they escaped into the land of Ararat, his son, Esarhaddon, reigned in his place.

Sennacherib was defeated because of the earnest prayer of the righteous; not one sword was thrown! This should give us hope that no matter what befalls or who is against us, God can deliver if we humble ourselves before His throne and surrender all the contents of our troubles to Him. Leaving all of the consequences to God provides an ultimate outcome and less injury to ourselves.

We see from the story of Hezekiah's prayerful faith that turning our enemies over to God allows an optimum outcome. Hezekiah sent his noble and honorable servants to Isaiah for prayers. He was well aware of Isaiah's exceptional power in prayer and his deep relationship with God. It's obvious from this account that Isaiah was a faithful and trustworthy prophet. Hezekiah didn't hesitate to call on his most trusted, God-fearing friends to help him.

We find that Sennacherib didn't just boast of his plans to destroy Judah, he sent it in writing! Hezekiah turned over the letter completely to God. He displayed before all that he wanted only God's glory and His Divine retribution on his enemies. Hezekiah acknowledged God as being enthroned above the cherubim, *winged angels*. God was not a human made god, but *is* Jehovah God, Who can only be reached in looking up to His Holy Face as Hezekiah did.

During a dark moment in the history of God's chosen people, God delivered Hezekiah because he prayed, turning his fears and worries over to his Father. It's further recorded that Hezekiah *trusted in the LORD, the God of Israel; and after him there was no one like him among all the kings of Judah, nor among those who came before him* (2 Kings 18:5). He was compared to King David. 2 Kings 18:3 reads: *And he did what was right in the eyes of the LORD, according to all that David, his father, had done.* While both David and Hezekiah were not perfect men, we can aspire to leave a legacy of faith like they did if we choose to love and honor God with our entire being.

Hezekiah knew his own frailty before God and sought to change it by making a choice to draw closer to God. Perhaps you have an enemy who seeks to harm you or those close to you. You may question whether you have the strength to find a way for peace or even doubt your faith because you have not lived as Holy and committed as you should.

If we are dealing with someone who threatens our security and safety, we'd also be wise to do as King Hezekiah and go to the LORD'S house, or our prayer sanctuary, and place our troubles on the altar for God to handle. And we'll see, as Hezekiah, that God will intervene in ways we cannot imagine or accomplish on our own. What a comfort we have knowing that God—Yahweh, the one true God—is able to deliver us in our time of need. And will do so while displaying His glory, strength, and faithfulness so that others may know Him more intimately.

Beautiful World

Nature allows us to enter her gates with a heap of
Worries and then to leave without any.

May the Heavens be joyful,
and may the earth rejoice;
may the sea roar, and all it contains;
may the field be jubilant, and all that is in it.
Then all the trees of the forest will sing for joy!
—Psalm 96:11-12

A few weeks after my brother's death, I was sipping coffee one morning when I heard a bird singing. I peeked out the peephole, so that I would not scare the bird. But I didn't see him, though he was still singing vivaciously. So, I opened the door to investigate the rapturous chorus, and there he was, a beautiful scarlet cardinal in the tree. He kept singing despite me being there and chatting with him. I smiled and felt just as happy as he was.

What I find remarkable about the cardinal's appearing is that I was thinking about my brother moments before the bird sang. The bird's jubilant melody delighted my spirit with joy and hope. I was shown God's magnificent beauty, consoled, and drawn closer to His presence that morning because of the cardinal's melodious appearing.

I experienced another remarkable bird encounter more recently. It was a late day in January, with misting rain, when I set out for a solitude walk at a park. With my umbrella in hand, I sauntered along for a few minutes of meditation with God and nature. My brother is often at the forefront of my mind, and this day was no exception. My heart filled with agony as I felt the crushing void his death had left me. I took it to the LORD in prayer, and while the words were still on my breath, I beheld a blue bird perched ahead. God comforted me through his little wings of splendor like He had done previously with the cardinal's appearing.

Everything that has breath
shall praise the LORD.
Praise the LORD!
—Psalm 150:6

But just ask the animals, and have them teach you;
and the birds of the sky, and have them tell you.
Or speak to the earth, and have it teach you;
and have the fish of the sea tell you.
Who among all these does not know
that the hand of the LORD has done this,
in Whose hand is the life of every living thing,
and the breath of all mankind?
—Job 12:7-10

Years ago I was walking around a college lake and observed a caterpillar crossing the path. I gingerly walked on by, careful not to disturb him. A couple with children were walking toward me. Concerned about the caterpillar being squished under someone's shoe, I kindly informed the people about the caterpillar ahead of them and asked if they would be careful not to step on him. I proceeded to walk, but looked behind after a few minutes and observed the family had done as I had requested; each peering down and hovering off to the side of the determined critter. I smiled and went on my way.

A few years ago on New Year's Eve, I went to Walgreens to pick up a photo order. As I was waiting for service, I overheard two cashiers discussing a mouse that had been captured after running around in the store. They now had my attention and I had to inquire further. I walked toward the women and there the tiny one was, nestled in a medicine bottle ready for his deportation. *'But he'll he get run over out there'* I piped, *'You can't release him on that parking lot, he'll die for sure!'* they replied, *'Yeah, you're right, but he can't stay in here! Do you want him?'* 'Yes, I'll take him,' I said, *'and release him in the wild.'* I paid for my photos and left with the baby mouse.

Upon arriving home, I told my family about him and we named him Micky Mouse because his ears were colossal for such a tiny mouse. I took him out of the bottle and put him in a tall plastic tote. I gave him some grains and homeopathic medicine to help alleviate any fear or anxiety he may have been experiencing. Then I knew I had to release him in the park. By this time, darkness had fallen as we traveled to a park nearby.

I carried Mickey Mouse to the grass, away from the road, and turned the tote on its side so that he would run out. But he didn't seem to want to go. I gently eased him out of the tote and returned to my car. As I sat watching him with the car lights shining on him, he still wouldn't venture out. I sat teary eyed thinking the poor little thing was scared, and in a strange way, perhaps felt more safe in the tote than in the wild where he would naturally want to reside. I knew I had to let the mouse fulfill a mouses' destiny and drive away. So that's what I did, I backed out and left him there.

> *He shall come down like rain upon the mown grass:*
> *as showers that water the earth.*
> *—Psalm 72:6*

Mown grass portrays pastured grass or pastured land that is sheared like sheep's wool. Like the nightly dew restores the consumed grass to a silken green, the Messiah refreshes our soul with vernal showers. His influence restores our souls with beauty and comfort that is lush with seed and fruit.

> *I went to the woods*
> *Because I wished to live deliberately,*
> *To front only the essential facts of life,*
> *And see if I could not learn*
> *What it had to teach,*
> *And not, when I came to die,*
> *Discover that I had not lived.*
> *—Henry David Thoreau*

Artists spend a lot of time using brush and paint to convey a mood or a thought in an attempt to evoke a passion dear to their heart. God is the ultimate artist and He has left us a beautifully painted portrait to behold each and every day. From sunrise to sunset, God's touches are every where; they speak of profound wisdom and beauty.

Many of us enjoy the crisp autumn season when the leaves begin to change with the promise of the season's first snowfall. Winter can appear dismal until we look up to the leaf-barren tree limbs and witness the red and blue birds still singing and nesting their young. Even in the cold, dark Winter, God's little breaths still sing and perch on the lonely limbs; the majestic chorus cheers our hearts with the everlasting impression of God's spirit.

The Bible is beautifully arrayed with descriptions of nature and God's creation. Proverbs chapter 3 tells us that wisdom is a tree of life to those who take hold of it. We love and admire trees don't we? They are canopies under a scorching summer and parasols from the pouring rain. The next time you see a tree, take a moment to reflect upon its designer and embrace His wisdom. May we let all of nature teach and enchant our souls.

> *And one cried unto another, and said,*
> *Holy, Holy, Holy, is the LORD of hosts:*
> *the whole earth is full of His glory.*
> *—Isaiah 6:3*

This Is My Father's World

This is my Father's world,
And to my listening ears
All nature sings, and round me rings
The music of the spheres.
This is my Father's world:
I rest me in the thought
Of rocks and trees, of skies and seas—
His hand the wonders wrought.

This is my Father's world:
The birds their carols raise,
The morning light, the lily white,
Declare their Maker's praise.
This is my Father's world:
He shines in all that's fair;
In the rustling grass I hear Him pass,
He speaks to me everywhere.

This is my Father's world:
O let me ne'er forget
That though the wrong seems oft so strong,
God is the Ruler yet.
This is my Father's world:
Why should my heart be sad?
The Lord is King: let the heavens ring!
God reigns; let earth be glad!

—Maltbie D. Babcock

Gift of Dawn and Twilight

*It is a good thing to give thanks unto the LORD,
and to sing praises unto Thy name, O Most High;
to shew forth Thy loving-kindness in the morning,
and Thy faithfulness every night.*
—Psalm 92:2

Each new day is a gift from God with a privilege to praise Him for being with us in the morning, in the night—every day. We are blessed when we praise Him in the morning. His presence will have a good influence on us, promote a cheerful heart, helping us to be pleasant, gracious, and kind to others, and preparing us for the trials and troubles ahead.

However, if we begin the day with a complaining or irritable spirit, we risk losing our peace, joy, and thankfulness for God's protection and oversight of us before the day has a chance to begin. Instead of a grateful, cheerful heart, we will be a miserable person through the day, and will make others miserable around us. He who sees nothing to be thankful for in the morning will see nothing to hope for in the day. Without gratitude, we cannot anticipate a bright future. Let us give thanks every morning for His mercy that has spared us dangers when we were asleep and defenseless.

Twilight brings with it stillness and serenity to settle us for rest. At the approaching darkness we can then reflect on what God has done for us through His abiding mercies and His loyal love. We can gather from His kindness in the past, reassurance, strength, and hope for the times to come.

> *If the day and the night are such*
> *That you greet them with joy,*
> *And life emits a fragrance like flowers*
> *And sweet-scented herbs,*
> *Is more elastic, more starry,*
> *More immortal, that is your success.*
> —Henry David Thoreau

Having a diary or journal, coupled with prayer, are beautiful ways we can focus on our blessings and help to clear away the days' trouble and insults. God is faithful in His promises, in His character, and in His in Providential care of His people. It is therefore appropriate to contemplate the faithfulness of God at the close of every day.

Lucy Maud Montgomery wrote, '*Isn't it nice to think that tomorrow is a new day with no mistakes in it, yet?*' Each day that we have to wake up is a fresh day, with a clean slate to start over and make it better than the day before. God's mercy helps us, His truth guides us, and together, both continually preserve us from sin and evil.

Before the close of each day, I like to think of God as the pages of my diary where I can express my feelings, failures, triumphs, joys, sorrows, hopes, and all of my secret thoughts and dreams. He longs to know our heart and has the key to keep its contents secured and protected.

> *But there is One Who made the constellations*
> *Pleiades and Orion;*
> *He can turn the darkness into morning*
> *and daylight into night.*
> *He summons the water of the seas*
> *and pours it out on the earth's surface.*
> *The LORD is His name!*
> —Amos 8:5

We Will Meet Again

*If I had a flower for every time I thought of you
I could walk through my garden forever.
—Alfred Lord Tennyson*

Scripture reassures that all things will be made new when we get to Heaven. Some of us ponder what Heaven will be like and if we will recognize our former selves and those we once loved. How is it possible that our former life, with its sorrows, will be wiped away? I've often reflected on my former pets and if they'll welcome me, along with loved ones, to the presence of God, Jesus, and the angels.

My dog was a central part of my world as a young child. He was my spirit's heartbeat and is treasured as dear family. I've often wondered, will I reminisce about his death and find that we were not alone the night we suffered a life-altering tragedy? Will I see, through the eyes of Eternity, that God was carrying me through it all and was touched as I drug my loyal dog to a barren place along the side of the road? Is it possible that I'll be given a glimpse back, perhaps a vision, of that devastating night and know that

God was holding me close to His breast while kissing my tear-ravaged heart? Then in a twinkling of the eye, will God raise my dog's essence to life with a new body? Will he jump up, excited to see me and lick my face, wag his tail and wiggle his eyebrows like he once did when we played in our broken world? I don't know if I'll remember my dog when I get to Heaven, or if I'll see him again, but I receive comfort in believing there's a joyful reunion awaiting.

The Bible provides some clarity on what we can expect from the other side in regards to seeing our loved ones. 1 Corinthians 13:12 reads: *For now we see in a mirror dimly, but then face to face; now I know in part, but then I will know fully, just as I also have been fully known.* The author indicates that we will see our loved ones face to face, know them and be known by them.

1 John 4:16 reads: *So we have come to know and to believe the love that God has for us. God is love, and whoever abides in love abides in God, and God abides in him.* We can also conclude that God is with the saved and those who suffer innocently in this earthly world. We are assured His angels are there ministering to them. I believe God's spirit and an angel comforted and stayed with me the night my dog met a cruel end.

There are times when we cannot make sense of tragedy; all we can do is press forward with the hope that it will get easier and will be erased in Eternity. Even though we can't comprehend what awaits us, we are assured angels and the Holy

Comforter are with the saved. Through our highs and our lows, God's arms are around us, His angels minister on our behalf, and Jesus, our Mediator, makes intercession for us.

Hebrews 6:18 assures us that it's impossible for God to lie and we can trust the hope He's laid before us. I Corinthians 2:9 reads: *Eye hath not seen, nor ear heard, neither have entered into the heart of man the things which God has prepared for them that love Him.* These words express the wondrous light, life, and liberty to those who believe in the LORD Jesus Christ. The things which God has prepared—in reserve—entitle the believer access to God's wisdom, His provisions of mercy, His gifts of eternal joy and happiness. These promises are included in the gospel and extend to all. In our earthly form we know God will take care of our needs, but imagine how much higher and purer the joys He will bestow in Heaven!

> *And God shall wipe away all tears from their eyes;*
> *and there shall be no more death,*
> *neither sorrow, nor crying*
> *neither shall there be any more pain:*
> *for the former things are passed away.*
> *—Revelation 21:4*

Wistful Portraits

It's completely natural and a welcome event to reminisce about those we once loved and are now gone. Our love for them, and their love for us, never leaves our heart. At any given moment we can settle ourselves in those quiet places and recall conversations—bringing to mind treasured words and moments shared with them. We can glean inspiration and encouragement from the reserves of our past. Most of us who have lost significant people have moments when we wish we could seek their opinion, talk with them about our troubles, or be with them just one more time.

I recall a time when I decided to downsize and get rid of some of my household items. As I was cleaning clutter in my basement, I reminisced over a large, unframed painting I had found at a local thrift store. The piece was quite old and a bit tattered around the edges. There was something about the vintage picture that captured my interest, so I purchased it. I had intended to frame the portrait, showcasing a woman dressed in a blue satin gown, playing a piano near an elaborate cascading staircase, but never made time for the project. So, along with other items, I placed the large picture in the collection for sale, not knowing a touching story was about to unfold as soon as the sale had begun.

A woman walked immediately toward the large picture, picked it up and asked, 'How much for the picture?' I replied, 'Whatever you wish to pay for it.' She was elated and took hold of the portrait, continuing to shop. After collecting a few other items, she was ready to pay for her goods. She then shared a story that touched me.

'When I was a little girl, this picture had hung above my parent's mantle,' she said, 'My house burned down, and along with it, this special picture. It is a copy of the same picture and I can hardly believe you have it for sale.' As she loaded her car with the rare portrait and a few other items, I said, 'My house also burned down when I was a little girl—I believe this is a God moment!' We smiled and exchanged appreciation for the gifts we had received in one another.

I later pondered this unexpected connection with a woman who had shared a similar childhood tragedy as my own. I believe when I purchased the picture, I was merely to be a keeper of the item until the shopper could find it. I believe we had come together in wistful portraits of time, through the Providence of God. Our journey in life isn't about the things we own, but more about the soul-touches that reveal a beautiful sovereign God Who dwells among us, orchestrating His Divinity.

Fountain of Youth

*Upon a beautiful face are the brush strokes of
Extravagant love, grace, and patience.*

Our society places a lot of emphasis on external beauty. There's nothing wrong with taking care of our bodies, they contain the temple of God after all. Some in society may jeer and cast out those among us who are physically handicapped, scarred, or who have physical infirmities that are not considered normal or aesthetically pleasing. And some of us may feel insecure in having a physical attribute that can't be remedied with surgery or medicines, but God doesn't view any of His creation this way.

Let's consider a man who is bald, but has a warm, most welcoming smile. Doesn't the smile triumph over the man's balding head? Let's also consider a toothless man or woman who flashes their radiant smile because they love and appreciate us. While we may feel bad that the person has a missing tooth, or doesn't have teeth at all, isn't their smile still dazzling and beautifully received?

Sincere and beaming smiles aren't made in a lab, they are outward expressions of a vibrant spirit—gifts given of God—and are priceless. Smiling isn't the only beauty we can exude with our lips. The words we express can have far-reaching influence on those who need a word of cheer, affirmation, or pearls of wisdom.

Years ago, I recall a lovely lady, a grade school teacher, who encouraged and inspired me with her beautiful timely expressions. She was warm, attentive, and lovely from the moment I stepped into her classroom. I found later she, too, had been a foster child and then I knew why she was attentive and approachable; she knew what it was like to suffer the wounds of rejection and loss. I have never forgotten her gorgeous smile, or soulful eyes, and the exemplary way she used her words to instill value to me, a broken and forlorn girl. She has remained as one of my greatest inspirations for kindness and grace.

Our eyes can be wonderful storytellers where a host of emotions flow. Have you ever met a person whose eyes helped you feel more serene, reassured, accepted, and valued? Love, compassion, acceptance, tenderness, and purity that exudes from within are attributes of God and remain eternal.

None of us look forward to getting older and it can sadden some of us to think of a day when our faces will be lined with wrinkles and our youth faded. I like to think of wrinkles and gray hair as brush strokes of extravagant love, grace, and patience. How can someone be more beautiful or handsome when their faces are etched in humility, compassion, and love? The next time someone extends the lovely attributes of God toward you, know that you have just come face to face with beauty that is exceptional.

In the end, most of us are not going to remember how beautiful or dashing people were. What will be most important is how others made us feel, and the impact their presence had during important times in our lives. We would do well to allow God to be our looking glass and strive to emulate His timeless beauty and immeasurable grace.

> *And let the beauty of the LORD our God be upon us.*
> *—Psalm 90:17*

Providential Gifts

I was reorganizing my house one day and came across a decorative wooden box. I opened it and found only a small piece of paper enclosed. *Today something you've been waiting for is going to happen*, was written on the parchment. I recall placing the cookie quote in the box, but hadn't given it much thought, until now.

Many of us have dreams and aspirations and if granted one wish, would choose for it to be fulfilled. We don't have to rely on a wishing well, a fortune cookie, or the candles on a birthday cake as reassurance our dreams will be fulfilled. We're promised blessings and gifts when we're held in the hand of God.

> I wait for the LORD, my soul waits,
> and in His Word I hope;
> my soul waits for the LORD
> more than watchmen for the morning,
> more than watchmen for the morning.
> —Psalm 130:5-6

The Scripture above conveys the psalmist encouraging himself to trust in God and to wait for

Him. He depends upon God and expects relief and comfort; believing it will come, longing for it, patiently watching for it. He trusts that God will provide gifts of His grace through His Providential power.

God's Word is the foundation for the writer's hope. He doesn't rely upon his own imaginations and desires, but instead on God's plans and desires for him. Can we also be sure that God will return in the morning with mercy in His hand for us? Absolutely!

> *You are a hiding place for me;*
> *You preserve me from trouble.*
> *You surround me with*
> *shouts of deliverance, Selah.*
> *—Psalm 32:7*

The Scripture above is a great source of reassurance and comfort. God is our hiding place, our city of refuge, an impenetrable wall where we are concealed from our enemies. And like the Psalmist, we can also feel encompassed with songs of deliverance while being confident of our safety.

Ephesians 3:20 reads: *Now to Him who is able to do far more abundantly beyond all that we ask or think, according to the power that works within us.* God desires to bless us with His absolute best. Housed within the soul of the saved is the Holy Spirit; working to expel evil, purifying and refining affections and desires, and ultimately, implanting good.

Despite what's happening in our lives or what's lacking, we can know that as we open a new day to the LORD'S heart, we're sure to find the answers we're seeking, grace for our lives, and God's tender mercies unfolding. We can hope—with expectation—that He'll deliver as promised. God longs to fill our needs, forgive and help us out of any calamity, and to bless us with His extravagant love. His gifts fill our soul with joy and contentment like nothing the world could ever offer. I hope this new day wraps you in beautiful surprises of God's presence!

Eternal Friendship

I've secured your beautiful friendship
In the trinket box of my heart;
There it will be locked away forever
With memories dearest to my soul.

Life is sweeter when we have cordial friends to share it with. Like ointment and perfume exhilarate the spirit, so do faithful friends. They bring joy to our heart, lighten our burdens, and are loved as family. We can speak freely with our friends about all things and know they will offer the same counsel in return. They will want us to excel, and will do their very best to be the wind beneath our wings to make that happen.

Ointment and incense make the heart rejoice,
likewise the sweetness of one's friend
from sincere counsel.
—Proverbs 27:9

When one friend is weak in an area of their character God sends a companion friend who can complement the other. God will not ask us to do something without the strength and the people to accomplish it. We learn from the example of Moses and Aaron in the book of Exodus that God supplies our every need to help fulfill what He has asked.

Moses had a fear of speaking, despite being a wonderful leader. When God asked him to speak to Pharaoh, he requested that God not send him. Moses expressed he was not eloquent and was slow in speech. And even with Moses' reluctance, God still instructed him to go, and further assured that He would help him and teach him what to say. Still, Moses asked the LORD to send someone else.

I love what God said to Moses about Aaron. Exodus 4:14-16 reads: *Then the anger of the LORD was kindled against Moses and He said, 'Is there not Aaron, your brother, the Levite? I know that he can speak well. Behold, he is coming out to meet you, and when he sees you, he will be glad in his heart. You shall speak to him and put the words in his mouth, and I will be with your mouth and with his mouth and will teach you both what to do. He shall speak for you to the people, and he shall be your mouth, and you shall be as God to him.'* None of us are alone in our lives to serve God. He's always there and has made the provisions ahead of time. He does thoughtful and mighty works through us.

Even though God was disappointed that Moses refused to take on the task alone, He extended mercy to Moses when He sent Aaron on his behalf. Because Aaron and Moses had a solid relationship and a loyal friendship, they were able to face Pharaoh and eventually lead the people out of Israel.

When God sends friends on a mission, and they are determined to carry it through, nothing can stop them, though independently each may struggle with weakness or fear.

> *That their hearts might be comforted,*
> *being knit together in love,*
> *and unto all riches*
> *of the full assurance of understanding,*
> *to the acknowledgment*
> *of the mystery of God,*
> *and of the Father, and of Christ.*
> —Colossians 2:2

When Christians are one and united in the love of God, their souls are comforted with Heaven's affection. There's no truer friendship than that of being bonded in the Spirit of God.

> *The next best thing to being wise oneself*
> *Is to live in a circle of those who are.*
> —C.S Lewis

Having friends who are loyal and honest with integrity can be a great source of encouragement and help in times of suffering. Faithful friends listen empathically, support and honor our dreams and aspirations, and love us with a guileless heart, while allowing space for us to be our authentic selves.

Friendship bonding often takes place between two or more people who are not entirely put together separately. Weakness and vulnerability are often the glue that creates the strongest bonds. When damaged and hurt people come together, there's a comradery to build support upon. Attempting to be perfect and polished can discourage others from reaching out and connecting.

True friends are those who are there when we've made a mess of our life. We won't have to summon or beg them to help us, they'll just know with their senses that we need them. At all hours of the night we can call on them, not only for emergencies, but even if we are lonely and just need to talk. They will encourage our spirit to be all that we can be. If we are down on ourselves and our value is obscured by the bitter blows of discouragement, defeat, and disappointment, they will remind us of our value and show us, with words of affirmation, the jewel we are in the eyes of the LORD.

Unlike Job's friends recorded in the Bible, loyal friends won't beat us down further by questioning our integrity and having perceptions that don't line up with God's view of us and the circumstances. They won't remain silent, saying nothing, when we're wounded and left berating ourselves from our mistakes or trials. No, they will remain at our side with words of affirmation and heart-felt consolation. They will use whatever means possible to help us find a solution for the burdens overwhelming. And there's always a big hug waiting no matter the season of life we're experiencing.

Through all weather, our truest friends are 'for us'. If you do not have such a friend, reach out and surround yourself with supportive, validating, and spiritually passionate people. Ask God to lead you to them as you seek more of His heart and His holiness.

Spiritual and emotional connections
Are the strands
That weave a beautiful bond
Of friendship and family.

Greater love has no one than this,
that a person will lay down his life
for his friends.
—John 15:13

Jesus not only gave His life for His friends, but He also died for His enemies. God, our heavenly Friend, is the truest, most revered Friend of all. When we put on God's loveliness and discretion—His essence—we are guarded and protected with understanding far greater than what our earthly friends can provide.

Empathy

I think you may be a kindred spirit after all.
—Marilla Cuthbert

There are many touching scenes and endearing characters in Lucy Maud Montgomery's novel, *Anne of Green Gables*. Matthew Cuthbert, a beloved character, arrived at the train station in the city of Avonlea to pick up an orphaned boy sent to help him and his sister, Marilla, on their farm. Matthew was surprised to find, however, that a girl, Anne Shirley, was sent instead. He never let on to the orphan that there had been a mistake, instead, he apologized for arriving late. They then left on a horse-drawn buggy to Green Gables where Marilla waited.

Even though there had been a mix-up about the gender of the orphan, Anne Shirley remained with the Cuthberts for the remainder of her childhood. From the moment Matthew met the orphan, he was captivated and moved with compassion for her and her need to be loved.

There are scenes in the novel that evoke pathos. Anne desired so desperately to attend a ball with her new friends. Matthew wanted Anne to have the very best he and Marilla could give, so he purchased a beautiful blue dress with puff sleeves. When the moment came to present it to Anne, she wept because of Matthew's generous spirit and love for her. The scene is reminiscent of a tender father and daughter affection.

As the story advances, Matthew collapsed in the field while Anne was nearby. She ran to him and cradled his head in her arms, and said, *'If I'd been the boy you sent for, I could have spared you in so many ways.'* With faint breath, Matthew replied, *'I never wanted a boy, I only wanted you from the first day. Don't ever change, I love my little girl . . . I'm so proud of my little girl.'* The connection we witness in these two characters creates a cathartic response, an unforgettable blend of love and loss.

Matthew knew how to nurture Anne's vulnerable heart and he loved her with everything he had. If we have been loved like this then we know how difficult it is to say goodbye as Anne had done when Matthew died. We also know that to have been loved like Anne is to have been granted a portion of Eternity that can never be taken from us. God is love and love is immortal.

Matthew's character was that of a quiet nature who exemplified empathy. His empathetic heart and Anne's deep need to love and be loved is what formed the tender bond between them. He was moved within his soul to defend and protect her because he could see deeper than the surface and what she truly needed. And perhaps there was a part of him that needed her.

Empathy is a more active response to understanding and helping others than just merely having compassion and sympathy. But all three attributes are important to our well-being, however. Matthew and Marilla had all three traits when it came to helping the orphan to feel loved with a family who would never abandon her. Of the two characters, it was Matthew who doled out all three without thinking twice. Marilla saw her brother's example of this, and in time grew to see he was far more understanding of Anne's initial pain than anyone. Upon Matthew's death, Marilla and Anne loved one another more deeply. They found solace as they lived in the memory and example of Matthew's unguarded heart.

When we receive an empathetic response from another we know that the giver has been real and thoughtfully earnest toward us. The Cuthberts, as well as the character Diana Barry, Anne's new bosom friend, were allowed to see Anne's vulnerable feelings, often raw and exposed. All three, especially Matthew and Diana, honored Anne's feelings and genuinely sought to accept her, making sure to instill value and love along the way.

All any of us want when we share our raw feelings is empathy. Bestowing empathy creates a bond that fosters a sense of belonging. And when we receive that support, we garner strength and resolve; confidence in ourselves that enables us to rise to our greatest potential. Imagine what the world would be like if we all loved with the same extravagant heart like the characters in Montgomery's novel.

God's compassion never fails, He's always ahead of our steps to make sure we have what we need and are never alone. God is the well by which all of us learn to love exceedingly. It is when we immerse ourselves in His Word, that we become transformed and arrayed in His awesome empathetic heart. May we fall so in love with the LORD that we cannot imagine even one moment without Him there to understand us, to walk beside us, and to be our *Place to Belong*.

To Belong

*I will put My law within them
and write it on their heart;
and I will be their God,
and they shall be My people.*
—Jeremiah 31:33

The Holy Bible contains the most magnificent love story ever written. The papyrus scroll tells of a Savior who lived flawlessly, loved endlessly, and died unconditionally for the whole world. The key to finding wholeness and serenity for our souls is to develop a relationship with Jesus.

I can recall my former foster child days and not understanding who the LORD was when my foster mother insisted I have daily Bible readings. Additionally, I was confused when I overheard my foster grandmother praying late at night to someone reverently addressed as *the LORD*. Who's *'the LORD', I can't see him, I've never met him?* I thought. Just because I didn't understand or know the LORD, was not confirmation that His Spirit wasn't in the room where Grandmother Ivy prayed.

I was once lost without direction until God rescued me and placed me among God-fearing women—my first Christian foster mother and grandmother. They helped to inspire a hunger for children's Bible lessons. As I learned more about Jesus dying on the cross for me, I, too, wanted to be loved by such a beautiful person. Then came the moment I recognized I was lost without God's forgiveness. I took to heart His command to repent of my sins, confess Him to all I knew, and then to be baptized.

> *Peter said to them,*
> *Repent, and each of you be baptized*
> *in the name of Jesus Christ*
> *for the forgiveness of your sins;*
> *and you will receive the gift of the Holy Spirit.*
> *—Acts 2:38*

I was elated with joy—joy like I had never experienced before my baptism. Suddenly fears, anxieties, and a sense of misdirection had also left me. It has taken years of successes and failures to develop the relationship I now have with God. Having seen life from two perspectives, with God and without God, I wholeheartedly choose God.

> *We were buried therefore with Him*
> *by baptism into death,*
> *in order that, just as Christ was raised from the*
> *dead by the glory of the Father,*
> *we, too, might walk in newness of life.*
> *For if we have been united with Him*
> *in a death like His,*
> *we shall certainly be united with Him*

in a resurrection like His.
—Romans 6:4-5

Though your sins be as scarlet,
they shall be as white as snow;
though they be red like crimson,
they shall be as wool.
—Isaiah 1:18

Seeking God with our entire being pleases God no matter where we are or how little we know. God met me where I was and He'll meet you too. He desires to heal the frayed and fractured areas of your heart and life.

When we're baptized, there's a supernatural celebration happening. God, Jesus, the Holy Spirit, and the angels, who abide in the heavenly world, are there with those who decide to surrender their lives into the hands of God. The angels rejoice while the Holy Spirit imparts Himself within the cleansed, born again soul. The indwelling of the Holy Spirit empowers supernatural serenity, discernment, and comfort. The old man of worry and sin is dead and forgotten forever. This is an astonishing moment for all who say, LORD, *I want to be Yours, loved and cherished forever in the Divine circle of Your heavenly family!*

Perhaps you've never known the LORD or had a close relationship with Him, it's not too late to develop one. God desires to be your *Abba Father*, your intimate authority where you are loved as an heir with God's Spirit. His love, reassurance, and Providential care are free to you now. He will give you pearls of wisdom, and His Son Who died for you on the cross, while leaving you with the Holy Spirit. If you wish to have a faithful friend in Jesus, an everlasting bonded family, and an eternal home, the Bible is your guide.

We have nothing to fear in this life or the one to come as long as we hold onto God the Father. Let Him take hold of your hand and show you His deeply devoted heart and His promises to you; you'll have a sacred sanctuary where only you and He dwell. Begin your life-changing journey with Him today—seek Him because He's seeking you!

Cherished and Chosen

*See how great a love the Father has given us,
that we would be called children of God;
and in fact we are.
For this reason the world does not know us:
because it did not know Him.*
—1 John 3:1

Some of us have suffered the loss of our families and have had to live without the sacred strands of bonded love. There is no higher love shown than when others adopt impoverished and detached orphans who have nothing to give them in return.

Our heavenly Father has adopted all of us as His children through His son. When Christ calls us, we become His brothers and sisters through His sacrifice on the cross. For God to accept us as His children—allowing us to address Him as Father and then giving us the inheritance of Heaven with all the splendor it holds—is a token of affection that rivals none other. This is quite extraordinary considering we are by nature sinful, ungrateful, and unworthy of such love and sacrifice.

> *But you are a chosen race, a royal priesthood,*
> *a holy nation, a people for His own possession,*
> *that you may proclaim the excellencies of Him*
> *Who called you out of darkness*
> *into His marvelous light.*
> —1 Peter 2:9

Peter, one of Jesus' disciples, tells us we are a chosen people—God's very own, His possession—belonging only to Him and unique by design. Christ set forth the church, the chosen, the one true family sanctified by His spirit. Through Christ's blood, we are no longer bound by our old ways of dwelling in horrible darkness, sin, and misery. His beautiful and enduring light cleanses us from all evil so that we stand before God, complete and Holy. We are a royal priesthood in relation to God and Christ—in their power and in their hopes and expectations.

No matter what you've done, God can wipe it away and call you Holy. No matter what others have done to make you feel worthless, unloved, or thrown away, God says; *You are my beloved possession—Mine—I will raise you up and never leave you.* With promises like these, we no longer need to walk around in darkness and shame because we have been called out of sin into God's light. We belong to the Almighty King—we are His royal daughters and sons, forevermore.

> *For the LORD hath chosen Jacob unto Himself,*
> *and Israel for His peculiar treasure.*
> —Psalm 135:4

God delivered the Israelites from bondage and brought them home to His heart. And God will do the same for us who are in bondage to sin and held captive to the horrors of this fallen world. This is such an amazing act of God toward the people of the Old Testament, and now to us!

When we truly accept and try to understand God's far-reaching love for us, we can't help but fall in love with Him too. Because He cherishes us deeply and has redeemed us, we owe Him all the adoration and praise our hearts can possibly give.

> *Now therefore, if you will indeed obey My voice*
> *and keep My covenant,*
> *you shall be My treasured possession*
> *among all peoples,*
> *for all the earth is Mine;*
> —Exodus 19:5

We are God's treasure—His costly possession—who are carefully guarded. And not because of anything we've done, but because we are precious to Him. God's love is deep and lasting.

When you feel small or unimportant, remember God has placed great value on you! You're value doesn't change despite how you feel about yourself or the circumstances surrounding your life. God says you are His precious child who He longs to defend and deliver. We are all jewels in His eyes.

> *Because you are precious in My eyes,*
> *and honored, and I love you,*
> *I give men in return for you,*
> *peoples in exchange for your life.*
> *—Isaiah 43:4*

We need only to believe in Christ, receive baptism in the name of the Father, and of the Son, and of the Holy Ghost to be a part of the one true family of God. Continuing to live a Holy life, while laying down our lives for the One Who has saved us from utter darkness, grants us the promise of eternal life with our Father.

> *But now, this is what the LORD says,*
> *He who is your Creator, Jacob,*
> *And He who formed you, Israel:*
> *'Do not fear, for I have redeemed you;*
> *I have called you by name; you are Mine!'*
> *—Isaiah 43:1*

Permanent

He restores my soul
—Psalm 23:3

We find in the Scripture above that David conveyed his ultimate trust that God would strengthen and renew his life and spirit. And even though our lives may not have turned out as we had hoped, we can still trust that God will restore our weary and sad spirits. We're promised lush green meadows to enjoy while walking hand in hand with our LORD along the lovely shores of hope. The Bible is full of text that reassures that if we remain committed and true to God's heart, not only will our life be restored, but our entire being. His heart is the fire that ignites our life, both physically and eternally.

My strength and my hope
have perished from the LORD.
—Lamentations 3:18

The book of Lamentations is a collection of poetic laments and was believed to have been written by Jeremiah, the 'weeping prophet'. Lamentations 3:18 records the prophet feeling defeated, isolated, and abandoned by God, but this was not the end for Jeremiah. With patience, and continuing to hold on to God, the prophet found a reason to hope when the light of God soothed his discouraged spirit.

When we consider the life of Job, he was not allowed to see—at the time of his great suffering—what we now know regarding his trials and the victorious conclusion God gave him. Another example of this is seen in the life of Joseph. His brothers sold him into slavery, he was falsely accused of a crime, and he was imprisoned. But Joseph remained faithful despite enduring abuse, slavery, slander, and the chains of bondage. God allowed Joseph to suffer in order to bring about His plans and purposes, and he used his brothers jealousy and wrath to help him save his family.

God wants us to trust and remain in His presence like Moses, God's righteous servant. God called Moses to lead the children of Israel out of slavery. But Moses asked God to not lead them out if His presence wasn't going to be with them. God honored Moses' request and remained with Moses and the people. Moses loved the presence of God more than anything and had cultivated a heart that was driven by God's timeless Spirit. He placed great value on what God had given him.

We see in the lives of these Bible characters that God turned the unfortunate evil and losses for their good, revealing His Sovereignty at the same time.

God does not allow a preview of our lives, only the days unfolding as we have lived them. Perhaps you, too, have felt defeated, slandered, misunderstood and silently cast out, or forsaken. If so, hold tightly to your faith like Jeremiah, and other great men and women of faith, remembering that your story isn't over yet. When we're honoring God's presence we are endowed with joy, peace, meekness, and extravagant love that's supernatural. God will reveal Himself to us and strengthen our hope through a graceful and faithful life.

> Then he said to Him,
> 'If Your presence does not go with us,
> do not lead us up from here.'
> —Exodus 33:15

Hang in there to see how the final chapter of your life is written because God's not done working on your behalf. Recorded on the pages of all of our lives are failures, discouragements, tears, fears, and lonely times, but none of it can defeat a faithful spirit nurtured and cherished in God.

> But this I call to mind, and therefore I have hope:
> The steadfast love of the LORD never ceases;
> His mercies never come to an end;
> they are new every morning;
> great is Your faithfulness.
> 'The LORD is my portion,' says my soul,
> 'therefore I will hope in Him.'
> —Lamentations 3:21-24

*And I will fasten him as a nail in a sure place;
and he shall be for a glorious throne
to his father's house.*
—Isaiah 22:23

The word *nail* in the Scripture above is referred to as the pins or large spikes which were used to fasten the cords of tents into the ground. In ancient times, houses were furnished with these large pegs, or nails and driven into the walls while the walls were going up. The strong iron hooks, or spikes, were worked into the mortar while it was pliable, and therefore used to not only hang garments and utensils on, but also to hold the walls together. It was also the custom to suspend these nails to hold suits of armor, shields, helmets, swords, and other items.

The description of the nail applies to a leader and assures that he will be safe and permanent in his plans and office. He will bring honor to his household, his kindred. Eliakim was compared to a nail in a sure place; all his family could depend upon him.

Jesus Christ holds the keys of the house of David and we, through His lineage, have the same reassurance. Our souls cannot perish nor can all that concern us fall to the ground; we are held up through our faith in Christ Who hung upon the cross for every one. He sets an open spiritual door to the believer and no man can shut it.

I know thy works, behold,
I have set before thee an open door,
and no man can shut it;
for thou hast a little strength,
and hast kept my word,
and hast not denied my name.
—Revelation 3:8

Jehovah God is an ever living God, therefore, He alone is imperishable. He promises the righteous everlasting consolation. We have a secure foundation, a home that will withstand all storms and where no evil can destroy or take it from us. We are permanent in His heart—our home. His magnificence is so lofty and high that when we finally do stand in His eternal presence, we will all fall to our knees in adoration. Some us will be on our faces, sobbing and grateful that God has taken our deeply wounded hearts—riddled with scars—to live forever as His treasured beloved.

But You are the same,
And Your years will not come to an end.
—Psalm 102:27

Loyal Love

*Steadfast love and faithfulness meet;
righteousness and peace kiss each other.*
—Psalm 85:10

*By day the LORD
commands His steadfast love,
and at night His song is with me,
a prayer to the God of my life.*
—Psalm 42:8

We're all going to be known for something after our life on earth has ended. Have you considered what you want others to remember about you?

Many years ago I heard the phrase, *I want to leave the world better than I found it.* That has always affected me and I decided I was going to work hard at leaving people better than I found them. When we consider the life of Christ, He was the epitome of this very concept.

Jesus took all of the evil and all of our sins on the cross, then died to leave a legacy of loyal love for us to emulate. In Him, we have something worth living and dying for. We don't always have to do heroic acts to leave people better than we found them. It can be as simple as leaving them with a reassuring hug, a friendly smile, or a warm hello. It's often the small acts of kindness that mean the most to us, isn't it?

Love is the greatest healer of all. We experience its power when someone speaks an encouraging word, does a kind deed or bestows a gift we weren't expecting. Those acts, whether great or small, help us to feel better.

Some of us are born in poverty and forced to endure the hard knocks of life. If you were an orphan, foster child, an outcast, abused and neglected, or a homeless individual, then you understand those wounds better than most. For some, family and home are only portraits in memory and echoes of a longing heart. Those of us who have gone hungry and not had our basic needs of love and life met have insight regarding suffering. Our wisdom and empathy is a source to help others. We can be determined to not allow others to suffer as we did and give to them because someone gave to us.

> *One who pursues righteousness and loyalty*
> *finds life, righteousness, and honor.*
> *—Proverbs 21:21*

> *But when the goodness and loving kindness*
> *of God our Savior appeared,*
> *He saved us, not because of works done*
> *by us in righteousness,*
> *but according to His own mercy,*

> *by the washing of regeneration*
> *and renewal of the Holy Spirit,*
> *Whom He poured out on us richly*
> *through Jesus Christ our Savior,*
> *so that being justified by His grace*
> *we might become heirs*
> *according to the hope of eternal life.*
> —Titus 3:4-7

The Scripture above is immensely comforting. Jesus is the love and the kindness of God Who manifested Himself in the flesh. We were not saved by works of righteousness we have done, but by the mercy of God. When we were lost in our sins, God the Father kissed our wounds, saved us, and made us whole to live with Him forever.

> *Your kindness has filled*
> *The rooms of my heart*
> *With exceptional delight.*

A merciful and kind heart who blesses and waters others will also reap benefits. We grow more peaceful and graceful with each loving spoonful we dole to others. God assures us that if we take care of others in their hour of need, He will take care of us in ours.

Passing on something of lasting value and being intentional and exceptional about helping to strengthen the next generation is a worthwhile endeavor. There are many opportunities for us to leave tokens of kindness everywhere we go.

> *A man who is kind benefits himself.*
> —Proverbs 11:17

I've often thought about faithful Christians who have died leaving a legacy of generosity and service to others. A cherished friend comes to mind now as I write this chapter. She spent countless hours knitting baby booties and hats for newborns at the hospital, donating to animal rescues, and extending acts of kindness toward people she had never met. Perhaps a part of Eternity is being allowed to see the faces of all the lives we've touched while we lived in our earthly bodies. If that's true, she has now seen all of the people whose lives were made better by her thoughtful and generous heart. She and her husband were grand givers. They gave to people who would never be able to return the favor, nor would they have ever expected it. Their loving legacy now lives on through their daughter's charitable heart.

Recently I was walking in my neighborhood and a beautiful black dog trailed alongside. The sweet girl obviously belonged to someone because she had a collar, but she didn't seem to mind joining me and keeping in pace with each brisk step I took. I chuckled at her enthusiasm in walking with me, and the fact that she had endeared herself to my spirit. She was an example of leaving others better than she found them! My spirit was lifted because of the dog's generosity in keeping me company so that I was not alone. As I reflect upon the Labrador, my heart fills with joy and I smile because of the enchanting time we spent together that evening.

Last summer when I was sitting at a traffic light, I saw bubbles floating out the window of a nearby car. I smiled when I observed the passenger in the car was a child playing with bubbles. Even a child sharing bubbles is kind and encouraging because it reminds us that innocence still exists in our difficult and struggling world. When others reflect upon us and our example, may we live in the grace of loyal love and a child-like innocence so that we will remain in the heart of God forever.

Who remembered us in our lowliness,
For His faithfulness is everlasting.
—Psalm 136:23

So we have come to know and to believe
the love that God has for us.
God is love, and whoever abides in love
abides in God, and God abides in him.
—1 John 4:16

Psalm 103

Bless the LORD, my soul, and all that is within me, bless His holy name. Bless the LORD, my soul, and do not forget any of His benefits; Who pardons all your guilt, Who heals all your diseases; Who redeems your life from the pit, Who crowns you with favor and compassion; Who satisfies your years with good things, so that your youth is renewed like the eagle.

The LORD performs righteous deeds and judgments for all who are oppressed. He made known His ways to Moses, His deeds to the sons of Israel. The LORD is compassionate and gracious, slow to anger and abounding in mercy. He will not always contend with us, nor will He keep His anger forever. He has not dealt with us according to our sins, nor rewarded us according to our guilty deeds.

For as high as the heavens are above the earth, so great is His mercy toward those who fear Him. As far as the east is from the west, so far has He removed our wrongdoings from us. Just as a father has compassion on his children, so the LORD has compassion on those who fear Him. For He Himself knows our form; He is mindful that we are nothing but dust.

As for man, his days are like grass; Like a flower of the field, so he flourishes. When the wind has passed over it, it is no more, and its place no longer knows about it. But the mercy of the LORD is from everlasting to everlasting for those who fear Him, and His justice to the children's children, to those who keep His covenant and remember His precepts, so as to do them.

The LORD has established His throne in the heavens, and His sovereignty rules over all. Bless the LORD, you His angels, mighty in strength, who perform His Word, obeying the voice of His Word! Bless the LORD, all you His angels, you who serve Him, doing His will. Bless the LORD, all you works of His, in all places of His dominion; Bless the LORD, my soul!

No Night There

In the land of fadeless day
Lies the city four-square;
It shall never pass away,
And there is no night there.

Refrain:
God shall wipe away all tears;
There's no death, no pain, nor fears;
And they count not time by years,
For there is no night there.

All the gates of pearl are made,
In the city four-square;
All the streets with gold are laid,
And there is no night there. [Refrain]

And the gates shall never close
To the city four-square;
There life's crystal river flows,
And there is no night there. [Refrain]

There they need no sunshine bright,
In that city four-square;
For the Lamb is all the light,
And there is no night there. [Refrain]

—John R. Clements

Coming Home

As soon as we're born we begin to die to this world, but as we grow in the wisdom and love of God, our spirits are renewed daily, remaining eternal. 2 Corinthians 4:16 gives that assurance, it reads: *So we do not lose heart. Though our outer self is wasting away, our inner self is being renewed day by day.* Just as we are dying to this world, we're growing more youthful with each spiritual birthday!

Our world places a lot of emphasis on aging and trying to turn back the clock. But Eternity tells us we're growing more youthful each time we praise, love, and honor God. Imagine what our first rebirth day in Heaven will be like; a grand celebration of exceeding and unfathomable joy!

In today's world, we're hearing a lot about the end times. And as there have been for many years, opinions and predictions are swirling. Some have been troubled by these opinions and are in fear of the LORD'S return. We are much closer to the end than we've ever been, that is certain. I believe we can use this time to prepare our soul and encourage others, then we'll have peace regarding our final hour.

Even though we often dread our death, many who have been at the bedside of their dying loved ones have observed gestures indicating angels and other heavenly beings were there to comfort and welcome them home. We all have to die to be reborn. My faith assures me that when we do cross into the heavenly world, we will never want to leave. Having fears about the unknown is normal in our human bodies, but God wants us to be at peace, and strive to our utmost to honor Him so that we can be loved forever with Him.

> *For I know that my redeemer liveth,*
> *and that He shall stand at the latter day*
> *upon the earth.*
> —Job 19:25

I often ponder what Heaven will be like when God's radiance surrounds our souls in infinite love. It's comforting knowing one day God will hold our souls within His being and we will be made new; wounds will be healed as our former lives, riddled with pain, loss, sin, and disappointment, will be wiped away. How God will do this, I don't know, but I trust that because He knows us intimately, He'll recreate us in beautiful ways we can't even imagine.

Think of the most caring, the most generous person you've ever met, that made you feel loved and valued, being with you in Heaven. I believe those attributes will be even more pronounced on the other side because worry, aging, illness, evil, and the stresses of this life will be over. Since we know from the Holy Bible that we'll be recognized, yet changed, I believe we'll be adorned in those essences, but their brightness will be more luminous, intense, and pure. Won't it be wonderful to spend all of Eternity surrounded by the pure, impeccable beauty of those we have known and loved? And isn't it wonderful that they'll be no darkness in Heaven, just one eternal blooming day? Imagine how magnificent it will be when our feet step onto Eternity's lush green garden and the Father's arms welcome us home *forever.*

> *How excellent is thy lovingkindness, O God!*
> *Therefore the children of men put their trust*
> *under the shadow of Thy wings.*
> *—Psalm 36:7*

> *May be able to comprehend*
> *with all saints what is the breadth,*
> *and length, and depth, and height;*
> *And to know the love of Christ,*
> *which passeth knowledge,*
> *that ye might be filled*
> *with all the fullness of God.*
> *—Ephesians 3:18-19*

We all need a home when this world has come to an end. Today is a gift from God, may we use it to prepare for Eternity. Together let's adore and honor our Eternal Father Who waits with everlasting love to bring us home. When we strive to be thoughtful, Christ-urgent people, while walking in Christ's wounds, each step leads us to God's heart—our forever home in His courts.

> *Give unto the LORD the glory due unto His name;*
> *worship the LORD in the beauty of holiness.*
> *—Psalm 29:2*

> *But showing steadfast love to thousands of those*
> *who love Me and keep My commandments.*
> *—Deuteronomy 5:10*

Our minds are a storehouse of our life's experiences, containing memories both grand and beautiful and devastating and painful. We'd be wise to sort through them carefully upon reflection, so as to not allow the cathartic process to steal our joy and peace. Let's resolve to be present for every day while reaching toward Eternity with over-flowing hope (Romans 15:13). And let us hold to the lit face of God so that we'll be safe and sought after, *forever*.

> *Thou shalt increase my greatness,*
> *and comfort me on every side.*
> *—Psalm 71:21*

Like the Psalmist, God offers us complete consolation. He is encamped around us and nothing can threaten. While we're suffering under a cloudy sky, God is working to increase our joy and greatness so that when the sun reappears, our joy will illuminate brighter and blessings will be more abundant. It's often during adversity that we're shifted to wonderfully uncharted seasons of refreshing and surprise. When our beloved Jesus was brought back from the depths of the earth, His greatness was increased and eternal joy was forever His. And so it will be with all of us who emulate Christ's example, remaining faithful through the stormy trials.

> *His loyal love bestows a garland crown;*
> *From ashes He has made beauty renown.*

Dear beloved of God, I pray your night is over and God has enriched your soul with strength as He has mine. I hope His Holy Spirit has comforted and soothed your heart. And I pray that if you did not know God's love before reading this book, that you'll embrace Him from this moment on. He's lovingly loyal to all who choose Him and honor Him. Oh, how deep His love is for you—may you fall in to His arms this very moment, He's waiting for you! Jesus is your Great Pearl; go gather His best.

About the Author

Teresa Ann Winton was placed in foster care when she was eight years of age. She uses her painful past as insight to help inspire and encourage others. The seed of creative writing began when she was still a ward of the state. Counselors and mentoring friends encouraged Teresa to journal as a way of coping with the complexities of her troubled childhood.

She published her first book, *Pieces of the Pearl: A Foster Child's Triumphant Transformation*. The autobiography gives a candid and personal view into the heart of a child who suffers a broken home.

Teresa has also published *Tears in the Lilies: An Inspirational Journey Through Pet Loss*, *Two Tears of a Heart*, *Impressions of Eternal Love: A Collection of Short Stories and Poems*, *The King's Son*, *Loved in the Locket of God's Heart: Devotions for Foster Children and Orphans*, and poetry at Crossway Publications.

In addition to writing books and poetry, Teresa has also published song lyrics. *Etched on My Heart* is a collaboration between Teresa and various vocalists and producers. Her lyrics express the heart's deepest hurts and life's greatest tragedies. The listener will find an empathetic friend in the songs' messages and a candle of hope to light their path.

Etched on My Heart is dedicated to orphans, foster children, and those who need a lyrical hand to hold. The album begins with lullabies written from the perspective of God as an adoring father watching tenderly over His children. The songs that follow, portray an orphan's heart after suffering the loss of family and animal companions. Concluding songs touch on themes of love, hope, and joy. Teresa closes the album with *Love Grows*, a ballad written to celebrate her son's birth.

www.ingramcontent.com/pod-product-compliance
Lightning Source LLC
Chambersburg PA
CBHW052140070526
44585CB00017B/1916